Christian Followership:

Discipleship and the Gospel of John for
the Post-Pandemic World

David E. Gray

Christian Followership: Discipleship and the Gospel of John for the Post-Pandemic World

ISBN: Softcover 978-1-955581-12-7

Copyright © 2021 by David E. Gray

All rights reserved. No part of this book may be reproduced or transmitted in any form or by any means, electronic or mechanical, including photocopying, recording, or by any information storage and retrieval system, without permission in writing from the publisher.

Cover Art: "Unterwegs nach Emmaus". Gemälde, 1992, von Janet Brooks Gerloff (1947-2008).

Parson's Porch Books is an imprint of Parson's Porch *&* Company (PP*&*C) in Cleveland, Tennessee. PP*&*C is an innovative organization which raises money by publishing books of noted authors, representing all genres. Its face and voice is **David Russell Tullock** (dtullock@parsonsporch.com).

Parson's Porch *&* Company *turns books into bread & milk* by sharing its profits with the poor.

www.parsonsporch.com

Christian Followership

Contents

Acknowledgements 6
Prelude 9
Overview 11
Introduction 14
Prologue 16
John 1 20
John 2 26
John 3 29
John 4 35
John 5 41
John 6 46
John 7 53
John 8 58
John 9 63
John 10 68
John 11 75
John 12 79
John 13 84
John 14 91
John 15 96
John 16 103
John 17 109
John 18 115
John 19 120
John 20 128
John 21 136
Conclusion 143
Epilogue 144

Acknowledgements

To the Gray children for the great joy they bring.

To Bridget for constant fun.

To all the members of Bradley Hills who model such faithful discipleship.

Prelude

If there is anything the pandemic of 2020-2021 has taught us it's that we are not in control. Who could have predicted the events of 2020-2021? A virus taking over so much of the world and our lives. The world was upended, changed, and transformed.

2020 was a unique year. A year of fear and isolation. Of physical and emotional trauma. Of protests and furloughs. Of losses of life and of jobs and of hope.

Covid 19 hit the world in a unique way. The pandemic challenged the world. It has been the most unusual year of challenge for us all.

We were in our homes, where for many of us, each day seems more similar to the last than different.

Some in the public health field have said this is the most significant crisis the world has faced since World War II.

It is one of those rare times in history where everything seems to stop for a moment. Where time stands still. Where we know we will look back someday and ask, "where were you when the Covid-19 pandemic hit?" Much like those in the past asked similar questions about where they were on 9/11, or when the Challenger blew up or when JFK was shot. Where was I? What does it mean?

Most American, and many global, schools shut in March 2020. Businesses, churches, enterprises, restaurants, gyms, closed to in person activities.

It felt like the whole world has gone on a retreat. Reflecting inwardly in relative isolation. How will the world emerge from it? Will we be different or the same?

Even as we begin to contemplate a post-pandemic world, we must be humble and realize that because we are not in control, we may take one step forward and one step back as we move towards the post-pandemic world. "Normalcy" may take a while yet.

This has been a time of great tragedy. So many of us have lost someone, or been ill ourselves, or feel the emotional, spiritual, or mental scares of this time. We may have lost a job, or seen our plans change. Many have watched school end prematurely or graduation ceremonies altered. Some of us has seen dreams seemingly die.

It has led an increased number of us to pray. We are praying for God's help. For safety. For healing. For job leads. For our politics. For hope. We are praying to God. Yet whatever we are praying for, this can be the beginning work for us of a concept called discipleship.

The pandemic reminds us that we were never in control. Discipleship is about us learning we are not in control, and, therefore, to become comfortable following. God is in control. We follow Jesus. That realization makes all the difference.

Discipleship is the practice being out of control. Of acknowledging and giving control to God. Of following, learning, and growing. Of learning lessons of receiving grace, accepting what we cannot change, and putting our hope and trust in something more secure, permanent, and unwavering than the things of this world.

The work of discipleship can be the work of this time. It can be what helps us as we emerge from the pandemic.

Discipleship means we become a learner. A disciple is a learner. Discipleship means to learn to become more like Jesus and to follow him.

It is my prayer that we will seek to learn to become his disciples.

Overview

When we think about discipleship, most scholars point to the other Gospels beyond the Gospel of John - the synoptics, Matthew, Mark, and Luke, rather than John's Gospel. We might think about instructions to disciples in the Sermon on the Mount, for example. Some say there is perhaps more action related to the disciples in the other Gospels and that discipleship is not one of John's great themes. Many books and articles are written about discipleship as it relates to the other Gospels.

Yet John's Gospel is underappreciated when it comes to the subject of discipleship.

John's Gospel has a series of "7's" in it - 7 miracles of Jesus and 7 "I am" statements. Here are 7 reasons to focus on discipleship in John.

First, there is a perhaps surprising listing of discipleship in John. For example, the word disciple is used in John's Gospel perhaps more than in any other Gospel. While there is debatably less scholarship about the subject relative to John's Gospel than the others, the word appears there the most, there is great interest in the topic in John. There are great examples of this topic in John's Gospel. The Gospel of John depicts a public Jesus in the first twelve chapters where he speaks and acts with larger groups. Then starting with John 13 we see a more intimate Jesus, as he moves towards his passion, instructs his disciples with his "farewell discourses," and both prepares for and experiences his death and resurrection. Within these sections, we see examples of him instructing his disciples.

Secondly, John's is the most recent Gospel, the last Gospel, the final Gospel, written. Most historians believe that Mark was written first. Then Matthew and Luke wrote their texts, likely inspired by a copy of Mark's. John wasn't written until closer to the end of the first century. There were fewer people around who had seen the "signs" or actions of Jesus. People around John's time were more like us, folks who had to rely on the words of Jesus written in texts like John's.

Third, the Johannine community was outside the mainstream. It was a community in the later 1st century that was developed at its own challenging place and pace. Theirs was a time where destruction, persecution and hardship continued in new ways, and where discipleship was more challenging as time moved forward when Jesus didn't return immediately as many expected. Later in time, without the excitement of being nearer to Christ's life, and written to a community outside the mainstream, meant that John had to start reflecting on what would happen if Jesus didn't return for a longer period, rather than more immediately. To deal with the longer period without Jesus required John to think about how Jesus' followers would act as disciples in their own community. Discipleship requires us to notice that things can happen over time. Change can be gradual and occur over time. Discipleship takes place over time.

Fourth, John takes a long-term view of history. We often think that people in the Bible of note experience immediate change. Like the Apostle Paul being blinded by the light on the road to Damascus and converting upon seeing Christ in Acts 9. So much charged in the spring of 2020 overnight. March 2020 saw restaurants, schools, churches etc. closing very quickly. John takes the longest-term view. Early portions of Mark's Gospel begin with the action of Jesus as an adult. Luke's with events around the birth of Jesus. Matthew begins with the genealogy of Jesus. But John goes back to the beginning of time. To God's creation of the world. The longer the term of view, the greater the perspective of discipleship.

Fifth, John has been called the most spiritual Gospel. The other three are more similar, but John just feels different. Just feels more spiritual. I am writing this as the world continues to march through the Covid 19 experience. We can't interact with each other as much during this Covid time. Many have been isolated at home. This is a time when we look inwards, with so much closed around us, we look inside ourselves. This is a spiritual time. So, the spiritual aspect of John fits the times.

Sixth, the ministry of Jesus itself in John's Gospel also takes place over perhaps a longer period of time, three years, than does his ministry as depicted in the Synoptics. Discipleship requires us to notice that things can happen over periods of time. Discipleship takes time. Discipleship is about transformation. It is a lifetime journey.

Seventh, John gives a glimpse of God that we need to hear at this time; this disrupted, pandemic-filled time. Of a God who is reliable, faithful, and worth following. So much is up in the air in our world during Covid. We need the high Christology of John. We hear in John of a faithful, reliable and powerful God. We hear that Jesus is divine. We need to hear that God is reliable, powerful, faithful, strong, almighty, dependable, and of the high Christology of Jesus. When so much else in the world is up in the air. We need John's Gospel.

As with the other books, the disciples in John's Gospel are easy to like. They have substance, doubts, and issues. They don't always jump right into discipleship. In that way they are similar to many of us. We resist the call. We don't always want to follow. We take our time in responding. It's like the sons in the famous prodigal son story. They are lost because they don't want to live in the father's house most of the time. They resist discipleship. We do too.

And yet Jesus patiently waits and calls us to himself. John's Gospel describes a variety of people who are like us. Who want to live life, to have a good, meaningful life, but too often resist God's call.

God is patient, and, as we shall see in John's Gospel, leads us to that real life by following Jesus.

There are so many great stories of discipleship in John's Gospel. In this work, we will lift up a lesson from each of John's 21 chapters that help us think about discipleship. We will end each of these chapters with a prayer.

I'm glad you are joining us on this journey.

Introduction

How can we learn to be a disciple?

I have a Doctor of Ministry degree in church leadership. Like many of my colleagues, I've studied what it means to lead a church, how to do it, and what resources to draw upon to lead.

There are many fields beyond ministry where being a leader is central to its training. I have several good friends who are experts in the leadership field. There are entire leadership academies and many resources spent each year on Americans becoming leaders. But we don't often learn about follower-ship. Where do we learn to be a good follower? It is its own area of study to be sure, and has increasingly some of its own resources, but it's less frequently discussed and focused on than leadership. A disciple is a learner. A receiver. A follower of Jesus.

Over the past five years, there has been a number of new resources being published about followership (See Amazon listings for faith based and secular resources about followership).

Learning to be a good follower is central to the Bible. We might call it discipleship.

Thoughtful discipleship means to be a follower of Christ. Jesus called his people to follow him by becoming his disciples. There is a call story of followership in each of the four Gospels of the New Testament. Jesus often literally tells his disciple to drop what they are doing and follow him, or to act as his disciples and they follow him.

In order to be a good Christian leader, one must first become a good follower. Discipleship is at the heart of followership. Followership is at the heart of Christian leadership.

How do we become a good follower/disciple? The Gospel of John can help.

Being a follower of Jesus does something additionally important – it gives life. Abundant life now and eternal life with God forever.

In John 20, John describes his purpose in writing his Gospel as, "Jesus performed many other signs in the presence of his disciples, which are not recorded in this book. But these are written that you may believe that Jesus is the Messiah, the Son of God, and that by believing you may have life in his name."

Jesus did many life-giving things, performed many signs, in the presence of his disciples. Those disciples lived during Jesus' lifetime. But we who seek to follow their legacy, to be disciples in our own time, don't have the benefit of experiencing those signs. Therefore, the Gospel of John was written for people like us, people who want to follow Jesus, but weren't there to see those original signs. People who desire to be his displaces so that we can have life, abundant and eternal life, in his name.

This theme is especially true because of Covid. As America moves through and, at the time of writing, begins to emerge from the pandemic, we are searching for life. Real, deep, meaningful life. We do so after a time when so much has been taken away. Following a period of more than 600,000 American deaths. So many job losses and emotional displacements. Following such a pandemic time, we are searching for abundant life again.

The Gospel of John can help us see how by following, following Jesus as his disciple, we can find what we are looking for. May this study bring us closer to God.

Prologue

John 1: 1-14 has been called the prologue to John's Gospel.

To be a disciple means to be a learner. We learn because God continues to speak to us through God's Word made flesh. Our savior, Jesus Christ.

John chapter 1 verse 14 includes, the "Word became flesh and dwelt among us." That is the phrase for us to hang onto as we begin our study, to hang our hats on, indeed, to hang our hope on. We are disciples of the Word made flesh. Of God still speaking to us.

Around Christmas 2020 I enjoyed listening to Christmas carols on the radio as I do each year. Several times I heard the song "Have Yourself a Merry Little Christmas" playing. You may know it, "Have yourself a Merry little Christmas, let your heart be light. From now on our troubles will be out of sight." Sometimes the radio plays the Frank Sinatra or Nat King Cole versions. Other times a more modern one like Pentatonix or Sam Smith or John Legend. One time I heard 97.1 playing a slightly different version which I had not heard before. Turns out the original lyrics to the song are not as merry and bright as what we hear now. Sinatra and others had apparently asked that the original lyrics be changed to make them more up upbeat and cheery.

The early lyrics for this song were written for and sung by Judy Garland in the 1944 film "Meet Me in St. Louis." The song first appeared in a scene in which a family is distraught by the father's plans to move the family to New York for a job after the holidays, leaving behind their beloved home. In a scene set on Christmas Eve, Judy Garland's character sings the song to tell her younger sister to just hang in there, to let her know things will be alright. Garland sang the original song, "Have yourself a merry little Christmas. Let your heart be light. Next year all our troubles will be out of sight. Have yourself a merry little Christmas. Make the yuletide gay. Next year all our troubles will be miles away. Faithfull friends who are dear to us. Will be near to us once more. Someday soon we all will be together.

If the fates allow. Until then we'll have to muddle through somehow. So, have yourself a merry little Christmas, now."

What a perfect song for 2020. For Covid. These original lyrics are appropriate, not only for 1944, and the weariness of World War II, but for the weariness of 2020. We were ready for our troubles to be out of sight too. We long for our faithful friends who are dear to us to be near to us once more. We longed for our troubles to be miles away. We hope someday soon we all will be together. Yet op-ed after op-ed in the New York Times and Washington Post told us it was going to be a hard winter to come. So, until the vaccine was distributed, we had to muddle through somehow. We had to just hang on.

On a Christmas night long ago, Jesus came to people who were just hanging on. To a young girl not ready to be a mother, traveling to an unknown town to give birth to that baby boy in a barn. Mary, who would see her son endure the pain of rejection, betrayal, and death. And came to a financially vulnerable carpenter name Joseph who was traveling with his pregnant fiancé carrying a child of mysterious paternity. They didn't even have a room to stay in. They were just hanging on. Yet they had enough. Through a pinhole of light, through God's amazing grace, the word became flesh that night and dwelt among them.

There is perhaps no better description of the incarnation of God than in John 1: 14's "the Word became flesh and dwelt among us." Verse 14 is what William Barclay called "the sentence for which John wrote his whole gospel."

The Word became flesh. This is the Word, the reality of God, which was there since the beginning. This is the glory of God. The action of God, the communication of God. The Word, which created the world and by its power continues to hold it, came into this world, to and for us. The Word came to make God known, so we could see in Jesus what God is like, to show us how God would live this life we have to live, and more. The Word, the might of God, came to show that God's power is stronger than any virus or challenge or division we face. That God reminds us that in Jesus Christ we are saved. That God's power came to help people like us. People who are just hanging on.

John doesn't just write that the Word came into our world, or became human, but that the Word became "flesh." That means to be vulnerable. For flesh is vulnerable.

We are vulnerable too. A friend pointed out that that it used to be that if you asked someone how they are doing and they said, "I'm hanging in there," we used to wonder what was wrong and would ask if they are ok. In the pandemic, if someone says, "I'm hanging in there," we think "yea, that's not bad."

At the beginning of Advent 2020, our daughters came with me to help me pick a Christmas tree from our usual place near the corner off Wisconsin and Bradley Blvd. We carried it home on the roof of my car, put it up and have been watering it each day. The problem has been that our stand was old and rather than going to Strosniders to get a new tree stand (or using fishing wire from my basement to hold it as some in our church Bible study suggested, where it would literally have been hanging by a thread), we used our old, and somewhat crooked, stand. So, our Christmas tree was leaning pretty severely to the right. My wife put a picture on Facebook with my suggestion that we put all the ornaments on the left side of the tree to try and balance it out. People began posting pictures in Facebook of the leaning tower of Pisa in reference to our tree. Our family began joking since we got that tree that we should place bets on what day in December we felt the tree will finally fall down and topple over. It was just hanging in there.

The tree leaning way over is appropriate for a year where everything is just a little off. One of our favorite ornaments hanging on our tree was of a trash container with flames coming out of it, with 2020 written on the bottom of it.

We had fun decorating our tilted, leaning, just-a-little-off own tree. Our family loves hanging ornaments on the tree. We put up many meaningful ornaments. One in particular caught my attention that year. It has two parents, Mary and Joseph, facing each other, and in between them is a baby in a manger. And all it says is "Love was born." Very simple. Very true.

The Word became flesh and it dwelt among us. The power of God, the love of God, became the dwelling of God with us.

The word for "dwelling" in the Bible here harkens to Hebrew bible prophecies in Ezekiel, to God's dwelling with the Israelites during the Exodus, and with Jesus later referring to the dwelling places of heaven.

To dwell means to remain, it means Christ stays with us. That Christ will hang in there with us when we feel like tipping over.

The song, Have Yourself A Merry Little Christmas, had one more change in the lyrics over the years. The lyrics today read, "Someday soon we all will be together, if the fates allow." But the original lyrics read, "Someday soon we all will be together, if the Lord allows," a recognition by the writer of the sovereignty, the majesty, the glory of the one we celebrate and follow as disciples.

The Covid time was not the perfect time. But God's love can be trusted in every time. We were hanging by a thread. But in Christ, God says, "Hang in there. I will stay with you through the night and beyond."

The most precious thing in the world to God, his son, came to save us. For the Christmas story is of Jesus, Immanuel, God with us. Love was born. The one in the manger was the Word made flesh who dwelt among us. And it makes all the difference.

So, as we emerge from the pandemic, we pick up the pieces.

We do so in hope and power, for the Savior will lead us out. The Word made flesh and came to dwell with us. To lead us. To save us.

We follow the Word made flesh. We are his disciples.

John 1

What is the invitation to discipleship?

The heart of our faith is that Jesus is our savior, our path to eternity, who offers us a right relationship with God now and eternal life forever. Our teacher, who offers us a relationship with ourselves, present, abundant life (our path to living now). Our connector who offers us a right relationship with each other and calls us together in the church (our path to relationship, communion with each other now), his church, empowered by the holy spirit. We respond by being his disciple. By experiencing him to experience what is holy and divine.

In John chapter 1, Jesus asks the question, "What are you looking for?" That is the question Jesus asks his two disciples. That is the question Jesus asks you and me, "What are you looking for?"

This is a fundamental question at the root of all we are doing in the church. Churches are broad organizations where many different people come together for differing reasons. Some come for the worship, some for the tradition they were raised in, some for the activities. Others for the music, or to give their kids a faith structure or for mission.

What are you looking for? This is a fundamental question at the root of all we are doing outside the church as well. Some of us in life are looking for power and success in career. Others are looking for a job. Some of us pine for peace.

Others want to be on better relationships with our family members. Some are looking to just make it through. Some are hoping to just get the world back to the way it was.

Others are trying to be a part of remaking the world. Others of us are hoping that our bodies just feel better.

What are you looking for? What Jesus offers is a path towards seeing something greater than we can accomplish on our own, than we could hope for, than we can imagine. It starts with accepting his invitation to reach out and follow him. We call that discipleship – the process of being a disciple, that means one studying the disciplines, that means being a learner, follower, student, pupil, congregant of Jesus Christ.

What does it mean to follow Jesus during, and coming out of, a pandemic time?

We think about these questions through the lens of the Gospel of John.

The path to discipleship begins with the question, "What are you looking for?" This year we answer, we are looking for help.

Whatever it is you are looking for, this year makes it clear that you aren't able to do it all yourself. This has been a year of disruption. A year where we are easily thrown off. A year where we know we aren't all ok. We are tired of watching zoom screens, screaming at TV screens when politicians said things we disagreed with, screening phone calls from telemarketers, and being scared that vaccines wouldn't arrive soon enough.

We need help. We need a savior. What Jesus offers is the strength, the rest, the holiness we cannot find on our own.

This year also makes it clear that there is brokenness in the world. Jesus offers is a path through the brokenness.

I enjoy playing tennis and one Wednesday I came home, tired from a match. I was carrying my heavy tennis bag with several racquets and balls in it and we have a storm door that doesn't open well. I pushed it open and it came right back down and crashed into my back and bag and broke the glass. Broken glass everywhere.

There is brokenness everywhere in our world. At Jewish weddings they break glass to remember brokenness in the world. This year we cannot forget.

Many of us feel overwhelmed trying to address the brokenness on our own. We are carrying a heavy burden. Jesus invites all those who we are carrying heavy burdens to come to him, and he will give us rest.

Others of us want to address brokenness and don't know where to begin. Jesus brings power and strength to carry on and address the issue we are called to address.

Jesus is not only strong, but he is holy, and accessible. He is the lamb. In the Middle East, sheep, lambs, were seemingly everywhere. Accessible and disarming.

Yet Jesus is not like every or any lamb, he is loving lamb. Lamb of God. Who loves us so much as to sacrifice and die for us.

It's not up to you to do everything on your own. To get work and school and home perfect. Or to remake the world on our own. I have lots of ideas in my ideal world, but John reminds me that I'm not my own savior.

John makes clear that Jesus offers a power that gives strength, rest to the weary, healing to the brokenness, and order in a time when all seems out of control.

When, in John 1, Jesus asked the disciples, "What are you looking for?" They thought about it and answered him with a question, "Rabbi, where are you staying?"

I don't think they were seeking hotel recommendations from Jesus. No, I think that what they were saying, is that they wanted to connect with Jesus on their own terms. They didn't want to answer Jesus' question about what they were looking for right then and there. They wanted to know where Jesus was staying, some Bibles translate it as, "where are you living?," so they could go see him when they wanted to.

That is a "don't call us, we'll call you" approach to faith that so many of us have. We say things like - I'll pray when there is a crisis and I need something. Church works when there are no sporting events on Sunday. Faith is an option if no one is looking. God works if life suddenly has an opening in my schedule. Let me know where you are staying, and we will follow up when convenient to us.

But Jesus isn't easily confined. He says to them, "come and see." On my time. You need to come now and follow me.

These disciples do deserve much credit in the end. They took the chance to reach out to Jesus. When they heard about him from John, they took the risk of following Jesus. Then when Jesus invited them to come and see what he was doing in the world, when Jesus invited them to come with him, when Jesus reached back, they followed him.

Jesus is ready for us to experience him too when we are ready to come and see what he offers.

The disciples in John 1 followed Jesus. They accepted the call to come and see and they experienced Jesus. Then they learned from and imitated their model in Jesus. To follow, to experience and to imitate Jesus.

The more time we spend with Jesus the more we start to grow to be like him. Notice in John 1, Jesus says to the disciples "Come and see." And then when Nathanial later asks Philip if anything good can come out of Nazareth, Phillip also answers "come and see." We can grow to be more like Jesus too when we come and see him.

We might say, well, that worked long ago that Jesus reached out to others, but Jesus doesn't notice me now. That is what the disciples said too.

Nathanial asks Jesus, "Where did you get to know me." Jesus answers, "I saw you under the tree." Jesus is out there even if we cannot always sense that. Even if our prayers seem unanswered. Even if God seems silent. Even when we wonder if he sees us. He notices us even if we may not realize it. He seeks to get to know you too.

So, go ahead and reach out to Jesus, even if you feel cynical or skeptical or unsure if he can reach back, take the leap of faith, and reach out to Jesus. He will go to lengths to reach back. He knows you. We may seem tired and too busy trying to deal with all we are dealing with to reach out. But reach out and seek to experience the discipleship of following Jesus and he will reach back.

I have a friend, a person who has gone through challenges in recent years. But one thing that has prepared her for the challenges of the recent years was the resiliency of overcoming challenges growing up.

When we were in high school, my friend's grandparents were tragically attacked and killed. My friend dealt with a lot trying to come to terms with her grandparents' deaths. As she went through her grandmother's belongings, she found her grandmother's diary from college. In reading it, they learned a lot about a very close friend of their grandmother. In her grief and effort to navigate through this tragedy, she did the work of finding the friend's address.

My friend took a risk and reached out and wrote him a letter to him to try and connect with this person who had been part of her grandparent's past. She wrote him a letter not having any idea if he would respond. She could have been cynical or skeptical or unsure if he would reach back. He did. He wrote my friend back, and shortly thereafter, came to meet my friend and shared his memories and photos of his time with her grandmother in the 1930's. He brought a box full of photos and mementos to share during that visit.

This began a friendship that lasted until his death many years later. My friend ended up going to the same college as where her grandmother and he had met. He and his wife came to her graduation and stayed in touch. Their correspondence was therapeutic and allowed my friend to know their grandmother in a way that they never would have otherwise.

My friend wisely wrote that, "In a time where the world seems incredibly unstable and unpleasant, finding these letters and his, act as a powerful reminder of how good people really are, and how something beautiful can come out of horrible experiences." That redemption is possible.

What are you looking for?

Jesus went through the experience of death so something beautiful could emerge. Life for us in following him. Now and forever. And Jesus invites, calls us, offers us redemption too.

The other question asked in our scripture is Who are you? Who are you? You are Jesus' disciple.

The invitation of Jesus comes to us in our brokenness and lack of control and offers us strength, rest, holiness, salvation, hope. It offers greater things than we can imagine. Greater things than we can do on our own come from following Jesus. Redemption is possible.

We have a legacy to inspire us. Our tradition offers the cloud of witnesses who have prepared the way for the Lord for us. Like John and the disciples of Jesus, those who have gone before us in faith, point the way for us to find the one who comes with strength into our broken world. Who comes to be accessible as the lamb and is interested in us.

Jesus comes to invite us to follow him. To come and see what he is up to. To accept his invitation to reach out, as he reaches back to beacon us to study him, pray to him, learn about him, lean on him, find our rest in him and grow a little more like him each day.

As Jesus' disciples, followers, and friends.

Let us pray. *Loving God, help us to follow you, find you and find our strength, meaning and purpose in being your disciples. Amen.*

John 2

One aspect of discipleship we might not expect to be important is humor. Humor can make us more humble, and humility is an important part of discipleship. Do we take ourselves so seriously that we aren't able to follow God? We should take God seriously, but ourselves lightly. As G.K. Chesterton wonderfully put it, "Angels can fly is because they take themselves lightly."

It can be too easy to be too serious when reading scripture. But what if we view the same scriptures with a humble sense of humor and joy?

There are "seven signs" in John's Gospel. Much like there are seven "I am" statements. The changing water into wine is the first one from John 2.

At first there seems little humor in the story. That is because we tend to view scripture only at one level, as serious. And certainly, it is serious, it's the word of God. At one level it could not be more serious. But I think we don't give God enough credit if our view of scripture is one dimensional. Scripture can be multi-dimensional. Not only serious, but funny and joyful too.

How do we look at scriptures? With a serious dour view, or a joyful view of God? It can depend on our view of God. We too often view God as a mean God. Jonathan Edwards and many puritans inspired a view of an angry God.

Biblical trivia experts are fond of saying that the shortest verse in the Bible is "Jesus wept." But there aren't any verses that tell us that Jesus laughed.

It's too easy to be serious at church. A friend once told me, "The ushers at a church I used to frequent saw their role as being serious and keep noise as low as possible. Two ushers in particular we called "Shush" and "Scold." They would wear serious suits that matched, often gloves, and keep the peace by keeping people quiet, especially children. We called them the "Shushers" because their only role seemed to be to "Shush" everyone. I remember one time when I was worshiping there, and I was scolded to be quiet."

They say laughter is good for the soul. We need laughter this year, need Godly humor this year, we need to respond to the pain and challenge at times with laughter.

I believe that God means for us to be joyful. God is the source of our joy. I believe laughter is central to our spirituality.

There is laughter in the Bible. Sarah laughed. The Book of Proverbs tells us that laughter is the best medicine. Many doctors would agree. Ecclesiastes 3:4 suggests that there is, "A time to weep and a time to laugh, a time to mourn and a time to dance."

We should acknowledge that joy is part of ministry. That joy is a holy value. It's a gift from God. In fact, the perspective of joy can change how we look at God. It can shift how we look at life. It can even impact how we read scripture.

Laughter can be holy. There are times when the Gospels depict Jesus as playful. Children wanted to come to Jesus. They were drawn to him. Children aren't drawn to people who are curmudgeonly all the time.

We can be joyful because Jesus was joyful. Over and over God has forgiven us. God's central quality is grace.

It's too easy to be serious in our world. But instead, what if we tried to be joyful and humble. This is what our world needs. In times of conflict in so many places, perhaps we all think about taking ourselves less seriously.

So how might we rethink our scriptures from a different lens, viewing God as multidimensional, as funny, and joyful?

In John 2, we hear the wedding at Cana story. Jesus may well have gone to the wedding just to have fun. In the text we read, not that Jesus had an agenda or went to impress anyone, but simply that Jesus and his disciples had also been invited to a wedding. Implying that he went for the fun of it. When the wine gave out, the mother of Jesus said to him, "They have no wine." And Jesus said to his mother, "Woman, what concern is that to you and to me? My hour has not yet come." That can be seen as a humorous line. Calling his mother, somewhat flippantly, and saying, why worry about that?

Then Jesus says a line he would later use in referring to his death or ascension, Jesus says to his mother, "My hour has not yet come."

And then Jesus' mom says to the servants, "Do whatever he tells you."

I have to chuckle when I read that. Sort of like Mary saying, "Uh, yea, he's kind of divine so do whatever he tells you."

One of the Great Reformation Confessions, the Shorter Confession, asks, "What is the chief end of humanity?" And answers, "Our chief end is to glorify God, and to enjoy God forever." It's not to be serious. It's not to be perfect. It's to enjoy God forever.

God is not a dour deity. Rather, God is a Lord of joyful exuberance. So, laugh along with your unpredictable, exciting God, and enjoy God now because one day we will enjoy God forever in the life to come. We practice that here when we laugh.

So, shout for joy all the earth. The angels sang when Jesus was born. We should sing and shout for joy too. We should come to Jesus like children, sing, pray, read the Bible, and approach God with a sense of joy. For in Christ, that is how God approaches us.

Enjoy the humility which comes from humor, and with it the openness to follow Jesus as his disciple. Let your discipleship be joyful and fun.

Let us pray. *Loving God, may your gift of humor inspire us and keep us inspired, so we can be your people. Amen.*

John 3

After a year of challenges, coming out of the pandemic, can we find a positive sense of new beginnings? For our country and culture. For ourselves and our families. For our time and forever. At a time when so much in our world seems stuck and in want of transformation, the good news of the new year is that in Christ, change is possible. For after it all, and after all, God still so loves our world.

One of the best-known portions of the scripture comes from John 3: 16. That God so loved the world that God gave God's only son. We hear it in anthems and poems. We see people holding signs with it at football games and at political rallies. Martin Luther called John 3: 16 "the gospel in miniature." It is a passage of God's great love. Yet this famous phrase can only be properly understood by examining its background and context.

It comes from a conversation between Jesus and a man named Nicodemus. Nicodemus asked questions. Jesus gave answers. Who is Nicodemus? Nicodemus was a Pharisee. He had status. He was called a "ruler of Jews." He was a member of the Sanhedrin, the Supreme Court of Israel. He had knowledge. He knew the law. Nicodemus was also rich. He had privilege. His name meant "victorious people." He had resources, both financial and connectional. He was cunning. He came to Jesus at night. His coming to Jesus at night was not only to be hidden from people. The Greek and the context lead many commentators to argue that Nicodemus came to Jesus at night because he was trying to hide from God.

Nicodemus was missing something in his life, so he went to Jesus. Because he had seen some of Jesus' miracles, he confessed that Jesus was Godly. He had some kernel of faith. But he is unsure, and perhaps saw Jesus as threatening. He went at night, traditionally a time people would do things they wanted hidden, including from God. And he says "we" know you are a teacher come from God, it's almost "as if he is saying I'm asking for a friend." That Nicodemus was trying to deflect attention from himself. Almost that he wanted transformation, but apart from God. I wonder what you and I try to hide from God?

Jesus says that the real change he seeks is possible, but only with God. With God all things are possible. What Jesus is able to do is to make transformation happen, to bring life, and real change. Jesus speaks of his kingdom.

We pray each Sunday, "thy kingdom come thy will be done on earth as it is in heaven." We long for God's kingdom. What Jesus tells us is that he can bring the kingdom of God.

Nicodemus knew he needed to change. His question was not whether or not he needed to change. His question was how such transformation was possible. Nicodemus questioned how Jesus brought about the values of the kingdom of God.

Jesus said one needs to be born from above. Nicodemus asked how that would be possible because one couldn't be born again physically. Jesus was saying that Nicodemus must start over – that he must be like a child again, to be born again spiritually, to be humble and willing to learn. A disciple. Jesus could do for Nicodemus what he couldn't do for himself. Be transformed, from the Holy Spirit, if Nicodemus was willing to listen and learn.

Jesus shifted the conversation. His point was that people can be reborn spiritually. Jesus can do so and for us what we cannot do on our own. In him, we can be reborn again spiritually. We can come alive spiritually.

Jesus is saying that to be in the kingdom of God, one has to reborn, that is to be a child again, a child of God, willing to learn, a sponge, vulnerable and humble, to follow Jesus as a disciple. Much like in John 1 when Jesus says that "for all who believed in his name, they received power to become children of God."

Such is the way of the spirit. We can't see it, but we can see it at work. We must and can come alive spiritually in our day and time. The physical change can come from what we cannot see – the holy spirit. This is a time in history when we must be clear on who Jesus is and what Jesus does. He isn't interested in being motivated by cunning, power and resources. We have seen too many use Jesus as a symbol of oppression to justify division, bigotry, and hatred. A Jesus we don't see in the pages of the good book, but on signs at riots. Jesus is not interested in justifying predetermined political outcomes or being used as a prop for prejudice, or as a symbol for posturing or as a way to provoke for its own sake. This would leave us staying mired in the hatred and disfunction that holds us back and bring no one joy. That is not the Jesus of John's Gospel. The Jesus of John's Gospel is about coming alive spiritually, honoring all people and seeing the best in folks, not the worst. Being transformed into our best selves. Our best culture. Our best church. Our best nation.

There is yet another interpretation of what it means for Nicodemus to visit Jesus at night. On slave plantations, many African America slaves were often not allowed to worship during the day as they liked. So, they worshiped at night. This passage suggests Nicodemus' timing shows that we can always go to Jesus, always find our transforming change, find a way, even when things seem against us. This is what it means for a person or an entity to be born again. We as a people need to be transformed by a new spirit. That is what Jesus offers Nicodemus. A new spirit is what is needed in our times now, now more than ever, as we confront so many issues, including racism.

Then Jesus shifts the conversation yet again. He looks to the things not here but in heaven. Jesus knew that Nicodemus was interested in what comes next after this life. Nicodemus had a lot going to on in life but got to the point where he was started thinking about eternal life. We all get to that point where we start thinking about heaven too. Jesus says, "If I have told you about earthly things and you do not believe, how can you believe if I tell you about heavenly things?"

Then he said, "No one has ascended into heaven except the one who descended from heaven, the Son of Man." Jesus is saying that Nicodemus with all his knowledge about the law and religion was a long way from the kingdom of God on earth, but even further away from Heaven. That if he didn't grasp what Jesus was saying about the here and now, he was never going to understand the more significant world of heaven. Jesus was saying that the one who knows about heaven is the one who has been there. The one who ascended to heaven is the son of man, Jesus. He is the one who had descended from Heaven. The one who helps us ascend to Heaven someday is the one who has been there. Jesus knows about getting up to Heaven.

But Nicodemus didn't grasp that as he was so focused on what he should do to get there. He knew he needed more. He studied the law. He had worked in the temple. He had developed resources. He couldn't figure out heaven. Something kept blocking him. Kept holding him back. Stood in his way, but he couldn't figure it out. He was working so hard to figure his way to heaven. Jesus was saying, I am the answer to what you seek.

One mid-November I went to my primary care physician for a routine appointment. I got the first appointment, 8am, and pulled into the parking lot at Sibley Hospital where the doctor is now affiliated. I went to the appointment, came out about an hour later, got in my car to drive home. As I always do, I had my parking ticket, I put it in the automatic machine where we put the tickets to pay. Then it asks for your credit card and you insert it and pay. I put the parking ticket in. It went into the machine, sat there for a moment, then the machine spit it out saying invalid. So, I took the ticket out, turned it around, and put it back the opposite way. It sat in the machine for a moment, the machine spun its motor for a moment but didn't seem to like the ticket any better because it spit it out again. So, I looked it a bit more, put it back in, thinking third time is a charm, and it went in and again the machine spit it out saying invalid on its screen. I looked at the ticket, not sure what to do.

By this time a line of cars had formed behind me in the Sibley parking lot to get out. And one of them began honking. Another person a couple of cars back started yelling something I couldn't understand. So, I tried putting the card back into the machine when the driver of the car behind me yelled, "hey buddy, the gate is already up." I looked and he was right.

Now in my defense, it was early in the morning. And I had just had blood drawn. It was a fasting appointment, so I hadn't eaten anything or had coffee yet. But the gate had been up the whole time. Apparently, it was a day or time when no one was working there, or they weren't charging. Someone else had paid. The gate had already ascended. I wasn't making any friends, so I quickly drove straight away and out of the lot and drove home. I was working so hard to figure out the ticket and was so focused on what I was doing wrong, that I missed the gift in front of me. Several folks at my church have had similar experiences.

There is change that lasts forever in front of us too. Because of Jesus Christ, the gate is gone, the gate has ascended, the gate to heaven is already up. Don't focus on what you have done wrong. The one who descends to help us is the one who pays the price, was willing to be raised on the cross, so that our imperfections aren't the end of the story. Jesus ascended; he was lifted up. So, the barrier which separates us from God is gone.

So that we can be unstuck and get moving in life. So, we can make it home.

There was more good news for Nicodemus and for us.

Then Jesus says the famous words, one of the most famous statements he ever made, "God so loved the world that he gave his only Son, so that everyone who believes in him may not perish but may have eternal life." More people have taken comfort in these words than perhaps any other.

When Jesus says eternal life in verse 16, Jesus means not only the length of life, everlasting life in Heaven, that is what is suggested in the verses before, but by eternal life he also means the quality of life. Meaning the joy of life eternal, the joy of knowing nothing can separate us from God's love, the joy of being with God now starts now. The verb tense of God so loved the world implies we can start the life, the hope, the reality we want, now. We can start enjoying life now. We are a people in need of transformation to something better, something positive and of abundance now. God grants us that gift.

I had a friend who shared that as elder at another church she was issued a key with all others in leadership to the library so that we could access the mailboxes and books in the church library. But she never used it because she didn't think she could get into the church itself. Not until she handed the key in at the end of her term did she realize that it also opened the doors to the church building itself...so that she could access the resources it held.

For too long, for too much of our life, we have been stuck and have settled and been divided, angry, frustrated by social distancing and being unable to be with each other. Waiting for things to get better. There are too many things we don't like about our nation and world. And yet there can be more change coming than we realize. There is no more need to wait, for good things can happen on this side of heaven. Now is the time.

For the message of the famous John 3:16 passage is that Jesus has already paid the price, covered the cost, for us. For three days he suffered in a tomb. The gate has been lifted. Over and over in the Bible, from Leviticus and Isaiah to Matthew and Mark to Peter and Paul's letters to the Romans and Corinthians, we hear of the servant, the Messiah, the Christ, paying the price for our sins, not so we could remain mired in misery and disfunction, or worries about our mistakes, but so we could be free. We don't need to wallow in anger or scrap to get by with unhappiness or be less than we can be.

Jesus' point is that there can be transformation and happiness and hope now. And after all that has happened during Covid, Jesus gives us good news for the new year. There is more abundance, more hope and more to look forward to in faith than we might imagine. Don't be so distracted by all the pain of the time, that we miss what we could be. As John 3: 16 makes clear, it is all a gift, a gift from God to us.

We can have intelligence and knowledge and resources. But if we lack faith, we can miss the mark. God so loved the world, so loves you, that you no longer need to wait for life to start. God gifts it to you now.

Don't you want to be a disciple of this kind of Lord?

Life can begin anew. The spirit is here. The gate is lifted. The price is paid. The gift of God's love is given to you. Receive it and be glad.

Let us pray. *Breathe on us, breadth of God. Help us to know we are yours. Give us the confidence to be your spiritual people, to know the barriers between us have been lifted, to live in gratitude that in Christ, for you have given us the gift of life, in the spirit, in heaven, in here, in heart, and in hope, now. And always. Amen.*

John 4

How do we keep going as disciples when things get tough?

John 4 tells us that Jesus went from Judea to Galilee, but to get there he had to pass through the middle region called Samaria. Often, Jews from Jerusalem would go to Galilee by traveling east, across the Jordan River, and up north and over, in order to avoid traveling through Samaria. Jews and Samaritans didn't mingle. They had differences ethnically, religiously, historically, competition and even hatred. Yet Jesus chose to intentionally travel through Samaria. He had a purpose.

We hear that he came upon a Samaritan woman at a well at noon. And he spoke with her. In doing so he crosses many boundaries. He, a male Rabbi, spoke to a female Samaritan.

That she was there at noon, the hottest part of the day, to gather water, showed that she was an outcast.

She kept emphasizing their differences. Jesus kept underscoring that they were similar. The most important thing about her to Jesus was not that she was a Samaritan, but a child of God. Last chapter we talked about a man named Nicodemus in John 3 who went to see Jesus at night. Jesus told Nicodemus that God so loved the world. That means even Samaria. So, Jesus went and spoke to this outcast.

Jesus asked her for some water. The woman talked about how the well where the water was, was deep. And indeed, it was. Historians have determined it was 105 feet deep. To pull a bucket of water, which weighed more than eight pounds, up 105 feet, had to be very tiring for her.

Jesus said that he offers her and us a different kind of water. He offers us living water. Water that doesn't go away. That doesn't end. It doesn't require a bucket; it keeps going and going. It springs up. It's renewing.

There are so many things we can try and satisfy ourselves with that don't work, that don't satisfy. But only Jesus quenches our deepest thirsts. He renews.

If I drink water here it will be gone. It could spill. It might freeze or dry up. But when we need to renew our strength, Jesus gives us faith. God gives a spring of living water that never goes away. This water is what will stay with us to give us stamina for the journey. The woman said she could give Jesus physical water, but Jesus said he had spiritual water for her which could quench her thirst.

In John 3, Jesus talked with Nicodemus about being born again. Nicodemus didn't understand Jesus, he kept focusing on what it might mean to be physically reborn. Jesus was focusing on the spiritual. A rebirth that could last.

Nicodemus was a morally upright, super religious, rich, connected Jewish male who visited Jesus intentionally at night.

The Samaritan woman was a poor, unnamed outcast of the disfavored ethnicity, faith, and territory, who had a chance encounter with Jesus at noon in broad daylight.

They were very different. Jesus loved them both. Both missed the spiritual gift that Jesus was giving strength that could last.

He was saying he had more to give them than they could give him. We affirm the truth of John 4, that we have more to receive from God than we have to give.

Each of them found strength in Jesus. The Samaritan woman left her water behind to tell her friends of the unique strength of Jesus.

Later John 19 tells us that Nicodemus left behind traditions to help publicly care for Jesus' body, to get it ready for burial after his crucifixion.

Both of them began to drink of the water Jesus offers. The living water. Both began to have their strength renewed.

Through their actions they made a confession of faith. They showed that they finally understood that their strength could come from the living water of Jesus Christ.

They both began to drink of his water. No matter who we are or what our background, Jesus can renew us and give us strength.

Now notice in their conversation from John 4 that Jesus is not afraid to ask the woman some very personal questions. Jesus says correctly, "You have five husbands." And she was also living with another man who was not her husband. She kept leaving and being married to five different people and in doing so crossed several moral boundaries. She didn't have stamina or staying power to stay with one person.

Though Jesus had never seen the woman before, he knew her story. God knows our story and is not afraid to get personal with us. And so, Jesus got personal with the woman at the well, as well. She was the only person in John's gospel to whom Jesus reveals he is the Messiah.

Jesus renewed her faith in God and herself. Renewed her strength. Renewed her belief that a real relationship, a lasting relationship, was possible. First with God, then with others.

I believe that is because she was honest about her brokenness and needs. When the woman was willing to be honest and confess her brokenness, she found the stamina, the strength to put her water aside, which represents her attempt to find satisfaction through the physical, which was one of her challenges, and she was able to focus on the spiritual satisfaction of Jesus' living water. When we are honest about our brokenness, we open our hearts to God's life-giving power, and we receive the healing of his spirit.

The woman was thirsty for a real relationship that lasts. That has stamina. That stands the test of time. If we are looking for a relationship that stands the test of time, that is what Jesus offers us.

Jesus says there will come a time when we will worship God not in a place, but in spirit. The relationship with him is not in a place, it is with a relationship that can stay with us. It can last.

I was so impressed by Capitol Police officer Eugene Goodman.

During the attacks of January 6, 2021, on the Capitol, when the rioters were closing in on the members of Congress, Goodman diverted the rioters from getting on the Senate floor. He got them to follow him up the Capitol stairs away from the members of Congress and saving lives.

He could have given up at the capitol. But he didn't. He could have fired at the rioters or used violence, escalating the situation, but he kept his cool. He could have run away, but he risked his own life. He was a black officer being followed by a mob of mostly white protestors carrying Confederate flags.

Rep. Charlie Crist from Florida introduced the Congregational resolution to honor Goodman with a special medal. Crist praised Goodman on the floor of the House for his "thinking and commitment to his duty and his country." Crist said, "While some will remember last Wednesday for the very worst in our country, the patriotism and heroics of Officer Eugene Goodman renew my faith."

Crist said, Goodman renewed his faith. This is what the living water of Christ does, it renews our faith.

Jesus says to us and all who are looking for real relationship and strength of the journey, I am he. I am the one you are looking for.

The prophet Isaiah said, "Those who wait for the LORD shall renew their strength, they shall mount up with wings like eagles, they shall run and not be weary, they shall walk and not faint."

Psalm 42 tells us, "As a deer gets thirsty for streams of water, my soul thirsts for you, for the living God."

Revelation 21 includes, "I will give you water from the spring of life."

Note that the woman at the well doesn't give Jesus water. He never ends up getting the drink. And in the next section of scripture he pushes away food. Jesus has reserves of living water to draw on. Draw on them. He has reserves of spirit that transcend the physical strength we have. He has stamina that is available to you and to me. Lean on him, draw on him, drink from him.

We need strength and stamina for the journey.

Sister Madonna Buder is a 90-year-old Roman Catholic Nun from St. Louis. She is a member of the Sisters for Christian Community. Several years ago, she was invited to give a talk at the dinner the evening before the competitors of the famed Ironman race were set to run the next day. Her comments before the meal stood out to many because she had real credibility with her audience. Nicknamed "Iron Nun," Sister Madonna was the 2012 world record holder in her age group and the oldest person, at eighty-two, to complete the 2.4-mile swim, 112-mile bike, and 26.2-mile run that makes up the Ironman Triathlon.

That evening her message was simple, "Tomorrow, when things get tough out there in the race, remember, you were loved into existence. If you get discouraged and want to quit, if you get injured and can't finish, if things don't go the way you hope even though you have trained for this day for months or even years, even then remember: You were loved into existence."

Sister Madonna wanted to remind that group of dedicated performers that the most important thing about them was true about them before they had performed at all.

The most important thing about you, before you get a degree or go to work, before you log on to school or achieve a success, before you shovel snow, before you go to the grocery or compete in sports or come to worship is that you were loved into existence by God. As we try and deal with the challenges of this time and try and keep going know that no matter who we are, from whatever walks of life we come, Jesus cares for us.

Jesus is offering you something that lasts, rest for the soul and eternal life. As a gracious, free gift. And so, you are invited to drink from the spring of living water that Jesus offers. You are offered water that can quench your deepest thirst for relationship that lasts. Living water that does not end. It can't dry up or spill. Water that can give you strength and stamina for the journey. So that you can renew your faith and your strength. So that you can run and not be weary. So, that you too can walk and not faint.

So that we can continue as Christ's disciples.

Let us pray. *Loving Lord, keep us alive in your spirit. Feed us and quench our thirst with water only you can give. Amen.*

John 5

Danish philosopher Soren Kierkegaard once said, "Life is not a problem to be solved, but a reality, even a story, to be experienced." That is true. The more we go through life we realize the truth of that statement. Life is not a problem to be solved, but a reality or a story to be experienced.

John's Gospel tells a story of a man with a problem. For 38 years he had a problem. He was hurt. He was in need of healing. In a particular pool, when the waters stirred, it was said an angel did the stirring, though it was more likely from an underground stream. It was said to have healing powers for the first person to set foot in the pool after it was disturbed. Kind of like in Shakespeare's A Midsummer's Night Dream, the first person to do something, in this case, enter the pool, had the special result.

There was man who for 38 years was hurt and not healed. The problem was that no one would help him get into the pool. Every time the waters stirred, and he wanted to go in, someone would step in front of him.

He found healing in the most unlikely way. Someone came along and told him to just get up and walk. He could not have predicted the miracle he experienced. This person who came along was Jesus. Jesus helped him. Not by getting him into the pool, but by healing him directly. Not by solving the problem of the line at the pool but by offering grace to the man, supernatural grace, that one can only receive, experience, from God.

This man's experience of Jesus took place in Bethesda. This is, in part, where we get the name Bethesda, the city of my church. There at a pool famous pool in Eastern Jerusalem.

There are many commentators who argue that stirred waters in the pool in Bethesda represent the waters of baptism. God stirs the water through the spirit to bring life to creation and to bring grace at our baptisms.

Many say John's Gospel was written by the "disciple whom Jesus loved." In the waters of baptism, we hear, as Jesus did, the promise that we are beloved of God. That is the core promise God makes to us. Part of our journey from that point on is experiencing and sharing that grace.

At first, John 5 passage seems a passage of independence as well. A man was ill for 38 years. Interestingly, Deuteronomy 2 implies that the Israelites wandered in the wilderness, not for 40 years, but actually for 38 years. So, for the man to be ill for 38 years symbolizes the wondering of the Israelites and of all humanity from God. Jesus asks him if he wants to be made well. Then Jesus says to him, "Stand up, take your mat and walk." At once the man was made well, and he took up his mat and began to walk. It seems that the act of getting up by his bootstraps is an act of independence.

Yet this is a passage of reliance too. Its second section is our hearing the man say that he didn't do it himself, but another person helped him, healed him. He relied on someone else to make him well. He just didn't recognize that man as Jesus.

When we join a church, we affirm faith in a God who can heals the lame, binds the broken, judges, calls people like Paul with flashes of light and raises the dead. This God can do miraculous things in our time too.

I would surmise that during your lifetime you may experience some of those amazing, surprising, and miraculous things, and just part of the challenge is to identify Jesus as our savior too. Yet God often works in many small ways too.

Most of the time in our walk with God we experience not fireworks, but friendship. Not phenomena, but presence.

One person asked me recently why God doesn't respond to us in prayer as directly as we'd like. Sometimes God does answer us directly in prayer. But sometimes, perhaps more often, God just sits with us. Yet as some of you discovered this year, friends who can sit together in silence and let their hearts speak, make all the difference.

Mother Theresa was once asked by a reporter, "Is it true you spend an hour each morning in prayer with God." "Yes," she replied.

"What do you say to God?" the reporter asked. Mother Teresa thought for a moment and answered, "Well, most of the time I just listen." So, the inquisitive reporter asked Mother Theresa a follow up. "Well, what does God say to you." Mother Theresa thought for a moment and replied, "Well, most of the time, God just listens too."

Part of our opportunity and challenge is to try and discern the presence of a God who is not always easy to identify. It wasn't for the man at the pool in Bethesda and it isn't always for us. Yet I hope you realize that there is a silence, a holiness, a sacred presence in prayer to which we can return time and time again.

In John 5, Jesus links his power to God's. Jesus says, "Very truly, I tell you, the Son can do nothing on his own, but only what he sees the Father doing; for whatever the Father does, the Son does likewise."

This doesn't mean that Jesus is weak. It means that Jesus is connected to God. In Jesus we see God. The words of Jesus are the words of God. Not from a posture of weakness but from the unity of love.

Our faith has a mysterious idea of the Trinity. Father, Son and Spirit. All connected. Reliance isn't weakness in the Bible, it's connectedness. This part of the passage emphasized the connected nature of God. Each part reliant on the other. And that we can experience God in different ways.

Relying on God through your life doesn't show weakness for you either. It doesn't make you week.

Relying on God will make you stronger, more resilient, more compassionate, more effective. It is the work of discipleship.

You can do amazing things too. But you do them best when connected with others. With God.

Life is not a problem to be solved but a story to be experienced, for the universe is not only your story. It's God's story. But you are an important part of God's story. You are beloved. You inherit a sacred tradition.

You are a disciple of Jesus. The disciples in the Bible learned to rely on God and each other. For they can do more together than apart.

As you walk the journey of faith know that everyone needs help in the body of Christ. You will find as you go through life and faith that you are stronger as a group than as individuals. That the whole of the body of Christ is even greater than the sum of the parts.

Each of us are spiritual, but we don't always realize it or have the vocabulary for it or think of ourselves as spiritual. We need the community to help us. For we are expanded by the experience of others.

You cannot do everything in your life on your own. But the good news is that you will find in this world that you have friends here. Most of all God who calls you beloved.

Once two members of our church were out in their truck and there was a dog lost on Bradley Blvd. So they stopped to help the dog, in danger running around on busy Bradley Blvd, and there they found their pastor in a kilt, there too, trying to help to corral the dog who had escaped from its home and was lost in the middle of the street. What was I doing in the middle of the street in a kilt trying to help save a stray dog? Trying to do something, anything, whoever small, to help heal our broken world. Well, together we helped return the dog to where it belonged. It was an interesting experience. But so is so much of life.

There are certain things which only Jesus can do. But we are not Jesus. But there are things we can do alone. Yet there are some things we cannot do by ourselves. And can only do with others. Or are better when we do them with others.

When a child is baptized, the church celebrates that they receive the gift of grace. Yet we spend the rest of our lives learning to receive it to nurture it, and to share that grace.

We spend the rest of our lives learning our place in God's great story.

Our journey to find our place in God's story is a lifelong one. The church gives us the language of religion to express our questions and confess our faith.

Christian Followership

Yet along the journey there may be times when we are hurt and need healing. When we are confused and full of questions. When we feel down and full of doubt. As John's Gospel helps us realize, only the grace of the Gospel, the truth of the Trinity, only the love of Jesus Christ truly heals. Even Jesus said, "By myself I can do nothing." May we remember that when we feel prideful or self-justifying or full of ourselves. Yet let us also remember that Jesus said, "With God, all things are possible." And in a world where thing seem broken, may that give us hope.

We confirm that when we rely on that Savior, on each other, on our tradition and on God, and take the leap of faith to walk alongside the God of healing, we open ourselves to experiencing the story, and in doing that, find our place in God's story.

For "life isn't a problem to be solved, but a reality, even a story, to be experienced." Many we remember that as we walk the road of discipleship.

Let us pray. *Loving God, help each of us, at whatever age and wherever we are on the journey, to honor our place and part in your story. Amen.*

John 6

One of the callings of discipleship is to try and be close to Jesus. We do well when we are close to him, and important things follow. Yet we are also called to get close to each other. For part of the work of discipleship includes caring about social justice and righteousness in our time.

In John chapter 6, John tells us that Jesus' followers did their best to be close to Jesus. Wherever he went they followed. Jesus went from the west side of the sea of Tiberias to the east, and they followed him. They went in order to be close.

For the hard work of racial and economic justice to which we are called, we need to stay close too.

The tradition of World Communion Sunday, a particular celebration in the Presbyterian year, in early October, began in 1933 to strengthen the unity of the church in a depressed economy and an increasingly fractured world. Presbyterians looked at the divisions of the world and selfishness that were prevalent, and dedicated a Sunday to promoting compassion, justice, unity, and a focus on the collective – the need for caring about that which is bigger than individual concerns. To try and keep the world together. The founders believed that if the world at that time was going to make it, to survive, justice and unity must be priorities. The unique message of World Communion Sunday is that we are all in communion with Christ and with each other. In a time of great division, it is about being close.

We needed that this Covid year. For we were separate. We were not close. We could not stand within six feet of each other. Even then we must wear masks.

This is a time when we need to try and keep it altogether too. For the world is facing significant issues.

Not only physical distancing, but we are facing significant political divisions.

We are facing economic divisions. We consider how the Covid crisis has laid bare the economic inequalities of our time. According to the United Nations, there are 925 million hungry people in the world. A third of children in the developing world go hungry each day. One in eight people in the world lack clean water. Nearly 15 million children in the United States – around 20% of all children, live in poverty. Morally we cannot ignore this. Theologically we have a call to care. Practically there are things we can do at home and abroad to make a difference, with our savior's help.

Jesus was interested in justice. People came to him to be fed and they were. John writes that when the disciples were concerned that they had nothing but five loaves of bread and two fishes, Jesus blessed the items and distributed them, and more than 5000 people were filled.

There are several interpretations of this passage. The physical interpretation - that in blessing the loaves and fishes Jesus transformed the food to become much bigger bread and unending fish. There is a sacramental interpretation. That the people were filled spiritually. Some of both is likely true.

There is also a social justice focus. That there was enough food already present to feed the 5000. The problem was people were not sharing what they had. As commentators have suggested, what was transformed in the miracle then may not have been the food as much as that the people. Jesus made it a potluck. They got close and shared their resources. That is a model for our world, where there are enough resources to go around, if we take justice seriously.

By the time the story ends, the people aren't just satisfied with filling themselves. Jesus told his disciples, "Gather up the fragments left over, so that nothing may be lost." They did not waste anything, but gathered the fragments of the five barley loaves, filled twelve baskets, which were likely given to those in need in the broader area. Some in life say the glass is half empty. Some say its half full. But the Christian agrees with the Psalmist who would say my cup runneth over. This is a cup runneth over moment.

We are at a time when nothing should be lost either.

To address injustice, we must be willing to get close. Jesus told the disciples to sit down, right where there were. Not get in a line to get food. Not go home. Jesus met them where they were. They weren't eating and running. He wanted them to stay awhile, be connected, be close. Note, Jesus came to the people. To each person.

John notes that Jesus fed them himself, he drew close to the seated people. John emphasizes that when they needed him, Jesus drew close. Close to this large, diverse group. He honored each person, of diverse backgrounds, made in the image of God.

This time of distancing, is actually a time for drawing close so that no person may be lost. This is a time in our history when we are increasingly aware as a church that too many people of color are not being valued. Too many Americans of color are being lost to joblessness and injustice and racial disparities in covid deaths and lost to mass incarceration.

We are called first to draw close to God, for our faith is a motivation for our work on economic and racial justice. Of the six great ends of the church in the PCUSA, social righteousness is one of them. We are called to racial justice work by the ends of the church, we are called spiritually to it.

As we do this work, we are called to draw close to ourselves. To reflect on our own journeys as it relates to race.

For people of color in our community, many have bravely shared experiences and raw feelings. We have had many people be part of adult ed discussions on race. We have had many people reading on their own. We have read and discussed books.

For those of us who are white, we have recognized and must acknowledge the privileges which come with being white and the burdens and inequalities which are part of a system and situation which is systemically unfair.

We also as a community I realize have lots people who care about the racial justice work that may not register in the church-based work. Who are doing this work outside church. Reading on their own. Doing racial justice work in their workplace or through their neighborhood. Or other organizations. Some have small kids and the timing is tough. Others are introverts and don't want to do zoom calls on this subject. Or would rather do some more action-oriented things than talk about it.

But some of us have thought about it, but for whatever reason, haven't leaned into doing the work of learning about racial justice.

So I want to talk, in particular, to people who look like me, people who are white, and, as there is a strong gender skewing of this work, those who are male.

From the three groups I participated in regularly in 2020, several 21 Day racial justice challenges; A Presbyterian Be the Bridge group to read and discuss these issues in every other week this summer and now monthly this fall, and from our South Bradley Hills neighborhood group. And from the activities our family has done, like driving the Harriett Tubman Underground Railroad tour on the Eastern Shore, I feel this work is important to do.

I've been trying to read more theologians of color, to quote more resources and references from people of color and to listen to views different from my own as a result.

We need to reflect on our experience and history too. Part of my experience these months has been reflecting on my own journey and past. We need to confront the reality of the world from which we came, and are a part of now, in order to make the future better. We need to get close to it.

As I've done the reading and participated in groups, differing memories have come to mind from my past. Reading and talking more about racism, both overt and subtle, allows us to confront examples we have participated in or witnessed in silence.

Some of the memories are hard to think about. The talk radio show we had on at a place where I worked where the radio host made a racist joke about gaining a holiday because of MLK's assassination, and what it would take to "get the whole week off." The coach on a sports team I was on growing up who channeled Howard Cosell's racist line when pointing to a player of color on the opposing team playing ours and called him a monkey as he ran. The summer softball team I was on in the mid 90's on

Capitol Hill, as part of the Tennessee delegation, when one team used a confederate bandana on the field as a base. And a friend of color looked at that base and gave a look of disappointment that pierced me to the soul.

Many of us who are white have had experiences that made us uncomfortable, but perhaps we couldn't put our finger on why it made us so. Moreover, we may not have had practice in speaking up when we saw racism.

The learning and reflections we do now give us those tools. Knowledge for what to say and not say. By practicing with awareness and compassion, we, and our society gain, as Brené Brown said, our full humanity.

I share my experiences with you to say that the work of reading and praying and reflecting on one's life in race is hard, difficult work, but it's important to get close to one's own influences and story, it's important to talk honestly about our experiences and about our collective history and it's important to be able to talk about race and the difficult things associated with it if we want to create a society where nothing and no one is lost.

Jesus wants to transform us too. So, I invite you to see racial justice work as part of your calling too.

It's important to do own work because one of the most important roles the church can play in my view is to support our members in doing our own work, for we all have a sphere of influence. If we shift how we view the world related to race, it can have a ripple effect on the world. This is hard work, but it is worth it if we have a better society as a result.

Then, I think we need to draw closer to a community outside our walls which challenges and expands our horizons. And I know some of you for whom talking about issues of race and justice is not as big a draw as working with a community on a project.

Jesus got close to others as he sought to make the world a more just place, and so should we.

Our family recently watched the film, Just Mercy (see his excellent book, Just Mercy, or Warner Bros. 2019 film by the same name or the Equal Justice Initiative).

It's the story of Bryan Stevenson, a Harvard educated lawyer who heads to Alabama to lead the Equal Justice Initiative to defend those wrongly condemned or who cannot afford proper representation. At one low point in the journey, Stevenson appears to have lost the legal appeal for a death row inmate and has indirectly gotten his son in trouble. Stevenson was down.

Stevenson talks with a coworker, played by Brie Larson. She had been trained that lawyers were not supposed to get close to their clients. But she says what she learned from Stevenson was that "You have to get close."

He was willing to get close to make a difference. It turns out Stevenson writes that he grew up poor in Delaware, but he remembers his grandmother telling him, "You can't understand most of the important things in life from a distance, Bryan. You have to get close."

For his work of racial justice, getting close was key. It is important for us too. We have to get close. The impact of proximity, the power of connecting, it impacts us too. In getting close we find the image of God in another human. We aren't as likely to stereotype or reject them as unimportant if we get close.

To understand our own story, history, and biases we have to get close. To be changed and change the world, we have to get close, heart to heart. We must take seriously what it means to get close. We must do the hard work of reflection and action that can lead to more racial and economic justice in our broken world.

Jesus got close. And so should we.

Especially in a Covid time, we must find creative ways to connect. This ministry of justice has potential to bring us closer together as well. Especially at this time of such distance.

In communion, we break bread together virtually and will celebrate our connectedness. Where through the Spirit, we seek to draw closer to God and each other. And to all who celebrate this sacrament in every time and place.

May this be a time when our work of discipleship includes our drawing close through communion helps spark our involvement in justice and our drawing close to our Lord, to each other and to our world. So that nothing, and no one, is lost.

Let us pray. *Loving God, call us to do the hard work of reflecting, studying, praying, repenting, acting, towards justice, staying close, so nothing and no one may be lost. Amen.*

John 7

In John 7, Jesus, perhaps reluctantly, goes to a festival of the tabernacles. He engages with the people. He shows great grace. Out of that grace came living water for those who would be his disciples.

One day we at church got a call from the production company of a show called The Real Housewives of Potomac. They explained that the show is an American reality TV series on the Bravo network, and they wanted to rent the church parking lot to film a scene for the show.

Now the Real Housewives of the Potomac is not a show I normally watch, so I can't really tell you much of what it's about.

Anyway, the producers explained that they had a change in one of their normal filming sites and they needed to tape a scene later that very day in a parking lot where one of the characters named Gizelle was teaching their teenage daughter, named Grace, to drive. They needed a parking lot for a driving lesson away from the distractions of a shopping center or school, and they thought the church would be nice, because it's easy for the 16-year-old, Grace, to get distracted, and not get engaged in the important task before her. Too often, for this self-focused 16-year-old, things were all about Grace. I'm not sure whether we would have allowed the filming but before we could contact our property management folks to make a decision we declined because they had to do the shoot that day and we had already hired a work crew that day to do work on the parking lot and front walk. But it was a good reminder to me that in our nation and world we all need to be engaged in the important task before us.

Fortunately, when it comes to our faith in God, it's all about grace too.

In grace, Jesus left the safety of Galilee and walked to Jerusalem for a reason. He could have stayed in the rural region of rolling hills and quiet hamlets near the sea. He could have stayed 100+ miles north of Jerusalem. He could have stayed in the relative comfort of Galilee. But instead Jesus came to Jerusalem. The capital. The city of David and Solomon and the temple. The Roman power. The arena.

Jesus could have stayed in Galilee, away from the needs and concerns of the world. But instead he got involved. He came to the place of challenge. He entered the arena.

One of my daughter's favorite movies from last year was Mulan. A Disney remake of a film of a female hero based on a book they used to enjoy. The movie was supposed to come out in theaters one year ago. However, everything shut down with Covid this time last year, so we couldn't see it in the theater. But finally, at the end of last summer, the film came out on Disney plus. And we were able to watch it at home.

The same thing with the musical Hamilton. They had planned for a movie of the musical to come out in the theaters, but, of course, Covid shut down the theaters. Our older two had seen Hamilton in the theaters, but our daughters didn't get to see it before it was postponed. So, they got to watch it at home last July 4 weekend. The same thing with Raya and the Last Dragon and several other films. We couldn't go see the films, so the films came to us.

We cannot get to God, to heaven, on our own. That why are in need of a savior. Fortunately, God came to us in Jesus Christ. We acknowledge our helplessness, our sin. That we need the creator to come to us. Fortunately, Jesus comes to save us.

That is grace. We can't make things right with God, so Jesus come to and for us.

In the Greek philosophical culture of Jesus' day, there was a concept of "Apatheia." It became of a goal in Greek stoicism to get to a place where one's state of mind was not stirred by passions. We get the English word "apathy," in part from the Greek word. Yet we are called by one who was all about his passion. Called to follow the light. To be in the arena, not disengaged.

The needs of our country, still reeling from the challenges of the past several years, underscore the importance of our reexamining not only our individual lives but our collective culture.

When we do that, we will find that are called to action rather than apathy.

Jesus comes to us so we can be filled. Not despair, but hope. Not apathy, but action. Not hatred, but love.

We are called to get in the arena by prioritizing our spiritual lives. To focus on his glory and in that to understand the meaning of his mission for us.

We get involved by taking care of our mental health.

Years ago, when Bridget and I were looking to have more space, perhaps start a family, we moved to near American University. When we trying to buy a home near AU Park. The area was great except that when we went to talk with the real estate agents, they said there was unexploded ordinance from WWI on the grounds of the house we were looking at. I was like "what?" As we came to understand it, American University used to test munitions in the area around WWI, and some bombs from 100 years ago could still be underground beneath my house. They found and dug some up in mid-September that year, I read. So that at any time we were going to start a family at any time there could be an explosion under our house. We had to be careful about what was buried underneath.

Part of the story is Bridget and I ended up buying the house in 2004 and lived there for 5 years and were always kind of concerned something would blow up. We had to sign a waiver/paper at closing saying we understood that there could be unexploded ordinance under our home.

If we don't deal with our stuff buried deep within us, it could explode at any time too. What is buried in you? What could explode at any time if you don't deal with it?

This has been a hard year. Mental wellness is really important. Many have called a mental health crisis the 4th wave of the pandemic. There are great challenges with grief in our time. Covid separation has made things harder for us. We all have some stuff we need to deal with. Don't overlook it.

Don't miss what is deep inside. Let the light shine on it. The challenges. But also, the deep longing of your heart.

Because of the passion of Jesus Christ, because Christ came to be with us, because God chose to come down and be with us, because of the sacrifice of Jesus on the cross, because of what Christ did for us this holy week, we are included in the real household of God, now and forever.

Don't be apathetic about your spiritual life, about God's love for you. Care about the needs of the world. Enter the arena of faith fully this week. Feel the passion that God comes for you this week. And give thanks that it's all about grace.

What can you picture right in front of you if you were too close your eyes? Wherever you are this day, who or what do you see when you close your eyes? What vision do you see? How do you connect it to God? What child of God do you see? How can you be involved in acts of justice?

Who is the person here in front of you that you are called to take care of now? The child of God in front of you?

Who is the person who is alone waiting to be called? Who is alone because of Covid and doesn't get to see their family? How can you reach out to them?

What are our opportunities to connect those different from us?

Who is new in our country, in our neighborhood, in our school? Who moved during Covid and is trying to fit in?

Who are the children of God in our midst of all ages?

Who are the missional chances for us to meet their meet with our chance?

What vision of the world do you see, where food, clothes, and safety are the norm for all, rather than the exception for too many?

Don't be so focused on or looking for what you are awaiting and what you expect to see so much that you don't see the deeper meaning or miss the person who is right in your midst. Right in your presence now.

Because we are loved by and connected to a gracious God. We are all children of God, and called to help the children of the world, rather than ignore them. We are called to justice with a child-like focus to dig deep to explore the needs, but also to see the opportunities right in front of us. The commitment to act rather than watching or waiting for someone else to do it. To see the light shine on us and everyone. To pay attention to the here and now. To love all children of God. To be positive with a purpose. For there can be a joyful calling in that.

As Jesus did on Palm Sunday, or during the Festival in John 7, or many other times, get in the arena. Be engaged. Care for yourself. And in the end, rely on God's grace.

Let us pray. *Loving God, help us to enter into your passion and feel your love, now and always. May we eternally rejoice. Amen.*

John 8

After the pandemic experience we have had, how do we have and where do we find hope? We have hope because God trusts us as disciples with God's light over and over again.

In John 8 we read, "Again Jesus spoke to them, saying, 'I am the light of the world. Whoever follows me will never walk in darkness but will have the light of life.'"

I enjoy receiving letters from members of my congregation. This year, with fewer in person connections, more folks have expressed thoughts through written handwritten notes.

One sent me a recent letter about Christmases in their childhood growing up in the Midwest in the 1930's. Born before the Depression, this person remembered a Christmas tree made of dyed chicken feathers attached to a stick and stand. How the ornaments connected and hung on the feather branches even with the star on the top. How the family would ride home from their Presbyterian church in a 1920's car in December to enjoy it.

My favorite description from their Christmas though was of their string of lights. They were a special part of the season. At a time when lights were not purchased commercially and weren't often used in their area at least, this person's family made the lights. Their parents made the Christmas lights out of old electric wires. Spaced apart with sockets and painted red, green, white, yellow, and white, these were special lights. Our member's father would paint clear light bulbs with a paint brush, and the lights shined the colors they were painted.

Each year they got them out for Christmas time. Over the years the lights got old, some parts broke, some wires frayed. Each year they weren't sure if they would turn on. The strand of lights was very heavy and a chore to put up. Our member said they must have weighed 100 pounds. But they trusted that the lights would work. And there came to be that moment when the lights were on the house outside and plugged in and ready to go. And they would flip the switch and hold their breaths and wait for them to turn on.

The story of the Bible is a story of God's light being trusted to our world. Since the beginning, the word of God was part of the God head. That word was expressed as light. The story of the Bible is the story of God not giving up on us but trusting us again and again with the power of God's light. And what came from that light was life.

The book of Genesis tells us that God said, "let there be light" and there was light. And light came into the world to bring life, earth, animals, and humans followed.

After human sin and the great flood, God trusted humans again with God's light and promised that God wouldn't cause massive destruction ever again, and so affirmed this promise with the light in the sky known as a rainbow.

Isaiah writes that God's servant will be a light for the gentiles. The prophet tells us that the wonderful child to be born at Christmas would be the great light to the people who walked in darkness.

Luke describes the light of God coming as that child born under a star.

In John's Gospel, light is a major theme, appearing 21 times. The eternal word of God would come as light. The light of God came in Jesus Christ. The source of salvation. The messiah. God trusted God's light coming in the world in the vulnerable form of a baby. God trusted the light to us.

And no darkness could put it out. Much like Isaiah described a people who walked in darkness, we face a dark time in history as well. This has been a difficult and challenging Covid time for us. And yet the good news is that the goodness of God is with us, during a challenging and dark time. The divine light of the word is the light of humankind, the moral light and insights and understanding that shines through the darkness of sin and mistakes. God does not give up on us but trusts us again and again. This is light in the darkness. We hear that the darkness could not overcome this light. So, we have hope.

John tells us that what has come into being was the light that shines in the darkness. Shines. This is in the present tense. But that the darkness did not overcome it. The darkness did not overcome it. In the past tense. Because of Jesus, the real darkness is behind us.

Despite all the challenges we face this year, all this darkness ultimately doesn't stand a chance against this light. God's light in Christ keeps coming to us again and again.

This light gives life. Life comes from light. Life at the beginning came from light. In nature where there is light, there is life, things grow. John tells us Jesus says he is the light of the world. He gives us abundant life.

With vaccines, there is light at the end of the tunnel. We can make it through. We can and must continue to be vigilant to make it through. But there is light at the end of the tunnel.

Jesus didn't come to remove all our troubles or fears. He came to give us new strength to make it though. He came so that we do not live in darkness. He comes to shine a light on our path. We came so that whoever follows him, whoever are his disciples, will not be lost, but found. That whoever turns toward the light will find life. Will find hope. Christ is the light of light. A light which flows from the love of God. This light and strength allow us to face our darkness and brokenness and fears and to accept, even celebrate, them, because God trusts us with the light.

In Jesus, God trusts God's brightest light to our world. And even if we ignore him, forget him, or crucify him, the darkness did not overcome him. The light rises every morning.

Advent begins our liturgical year with the light at the end of the tunnel. A baby born in a manger under a star as the light guided shepherds and wise men. Advent celebrates that Jesus will return as a bright light on clouds descending. God keeps sending us the light. Even when we break it, it comes again and again in grace.

The story is told that in 1879, Thomas Alva Edison made his first prototype Electric Bulb. He had experimented more than 1000 times over the past year before coming up with a working model. All his assistants were very happy that finally his research was successful. Edison then called his office boy and told the boy to carry the new bulb up to the testing site. Step by step the boy cautiously watched his hands, obviously frightened of dropping such a priceless piece of work. The boy was very nervous and while carrying the bulb he accidentally dropped it and it shattered. This great invention was in pieces. He was afraid that Edison might fire him from the job for his negligence. But Edison went back and made a new bulb. Again, he called the same office boy to carry the bulb to the testing site. All of the Edison's assistants were surprised to see that and didn't understand why he gave bulb to the same office boy who had dropped it before. But the boy successfully carried it, and by Christmas 1879, the first light bulb was ready to go. The assistants asked to Edison that why did he call the same office boy as there are chances of him dropping it again, and that all his effort would go to waste. Edison was asked about trusting the boy and he reportedly replied that "yes, it took many hours to construct a new bulb and if he drops it again, I can construct one again, but had I not given him the same task again, he would have lost his confidence, belief that he could do it, and faith in himself and hope which is very difficult to get back, and I don't want that to happen." Edison trusted his light to the boy. He entrusted his light, even though his mortal, imperfect assistant, had broken it.

God is our creator and inventor who entrusts God's light to us, to our world, over and over. Knowing we might break it. And we do time and time again. But that's ok, as Leonard Cohen sings, "There's a crack in everything, that's how the light gets in."

God rebuilds our lives, our confidence, our hopes, our dreams, our future, our belief, our faith.

So, during this challenging time, think about what light God is entrusting to you. To care for and nurture and love. What part of Christ's ministry is God putting in your hands?

What is God entrusting to you as Christ's disciple?

How is this light shown in your discipleship?

Just as we give parents a candle on the occasion of a child's baptism at our church as God entrusts an infant to them and to remind them that the light of Christ burns in each of our hearts, especially for a baby, at Christmas we celebrate that God's light came to us as a child. We recall that Christ's light can be the life for all people. Nurture that light. And if you feel nervous or fragile or broken, return to the gracious arms of the source of that light.

God has entrusted light to us. The light of Christ. The light which lives on from Jesus. The light of the world. The light that lives in our hearts. Which guides our steps. Which gives us life. Which gives us hope. Light which no darkness can overcome. So that of we, Christ's disciples, may became a light in and for the world. So that we don't hide our light under a bushel. But that we let it shine. Let is shine. Let it shine.

Let us pray. *Creator of the stars of night. May your everlasting light be our guide this day and this season and always. Amen.*

John 9

In John 9 we read, "He answered them, 'I have told you already, and you would not listen. Why do you want to hear it again? Do you also want to become his disciples?'" We want to be Jesus' disciples. We have to open our eyes, ears, and hearts to his grace in order to do so. Fortunately, Jesus can help us do so.

On a friend of mine's desk there is a little statue of three monkeys. One with hands over its eyes, one with hands over its ears and one with hands over its mouth. It is a copy of a well-known figurine called "see no evil, hear no evil, speak no evil." Or "see nothing, hear nothing, say nothing." The point is made in Buddhist and other religious traditions that it represents someone who has an inappropriate view of what is morally right. Either they dwell too much on negative thoughts rather than being positive. Or they seem to have overly positive thoughts and are looking the other way when something is wrong.

The Pharisees are guilty of both in John 9.

We live in a world where there are many things right and many wrong, and part of our opportunity is to try and attune our senses to understanding them. It's too common to have a misplaced focus on right and wrong or think those who have different views are necessarily sinners. But Jesus came to shed a light on all this. To help us sort this out. To allow us to open our senses to a better way.

According to John, Jesus once saw a man who had been blind since birth. His disciples asked him, "Rabbi, who sinned, this man or his parents, that he was born blind?" Jesus replied, "Neither this man nor his parents sinned," said Jesus.

Then, like God making Adam from the dust of the earth, Jesus spit on the ground, made some mud, and put it on the man's eyes. Jesus said, "Go and wash in the Pool of Siloam." This word meant "Sent." So, the man went and washed, and gained his sight. He was able to see. Jesus brought light to his world. He gave him a second chance.

This man was well known for his begging, so people asked, "Isn't this the same man who used to sit and beg?" Some claimed that he was. Others said, "No, he only looks like him." Both conclusions were correct. He was the same and not the same. He was like the same person, but he was also transformed. When asked are you the same person, he answered "ego eimi" - I am. The same response that Jesus often gave when asked who he was. The man had courage to affiliate with Jesus even knowing he could be in trouble for saying positive things about Jesus whom the Pharisees disliked.

The Pharisees asked the man how his eyes were opened. He told them that a man called Jesus made mud, put it on his eyes, and he was able to see. "How then were your eyes opened?" they asked. He replied, "The man they call Jesus made some mud and put it on my eyes. He told me to go to Siloam and wash. So, I went and washed, and then I could see." "Where is this man?" they asked him. "I don't know," he said.

The man born blind was now able to see. However, the Pharisees missed the moral importance of the event. They were the ones who were spiritually blind. The Pharisees could see physically, but not spiritually. They claimed to be religious but lacked the ability to see that God was revealed in Jesus. In some ways this builds on earlier stories in John's Gospel, with Nicodemus and the woman at the well, who focused on the physical and missed the spiritual aspects of Jesus' ministry. That in Christ, we can be a new creation by God's amazing grace.

The man born blind had a special sense of who Jesus was and so received Jesus and went out of his way to travel, blind, with mud on his eyes, to a special place in order to be saved.

The man born blind allowed Jesus to help him. The blind man does not come to Jesus or make a request for healing or have any conversation with Jesus about it. The man born blind couldn't see Jesus. He didn't know who he was. Yet he allowed him to rub mud on his eyes. Jesus said Go…to a place called "Sent," and he obeyed.

This is a call story. Jesus takes action, but so does the man. The man born blind was able to spiritually sense the importance of Jesus. The man born blind had a special sense of who Jesus was and so received

Jesus. He went out of his way to travel, blind, with mud on his eyes, to a special place, in order to be saved.

As John tells it, after Jesus healed the man, then the storm came. This often happens in the Gospels. Jesus had a way of getting under the Pharisees' skin. The Pharisees were furious that healing had been done on the Sabbath, so they spoke words of condemnation, prejudice, and judgement. Then they asked the blind man's parents who healed their son.

The parents pretended like they didn't know. But they had to know. The man had returned home, and his neighbors seemed to know, so his parents had to know the story. The man's childhood likely had some trauma to it or challenge for the parents, who had raised their child born blind, and one would expect them to have more excitement and interest. That they would have shared his joy. Instead, our text tells us that they were afraid. They are unwilling to say anything. They don't admit to knowing what happened to their son. They said, "He is of age. He can speak for himself." They said nothing, even to help their son. They were afraid the Pharisees would excommunicate them from the temple. So rather than protecting their son, the parents protected themselves. The Pharisees end up condemning and throwing out the son. The very punishment the parents were afraid of receiving themselves, being pushed from the temple, is what their son receives. And yet they don't jump into the conversation to say something to help him.

There are times when it's important to speak up.

This is a time when storms of division and hatred continue to swirl in our land. The January 6, 2021 insurrection at the US Capitol threatened lives and our belief in ourselves. There are too many prejudices and divisions and heartaches in society.

God does not mean for us to live this way. This is not who God created us to be. We are called to be better.

We are called to open our eyes to see the inequities, needs and opportunities of our world. Open our ears to injustices. And to speak up.

At this critical time, we who would follow Jesus, those who would be his disciples, should try and reclaim those habits of the heart. When we are tempted to exclude someone for being different, as the Pharisee tried to, we must follow the best angels of our lives. We are to hope and not to be motivated by fear like the parents. We are to cultivate the habits of the heart. We seek to open our eyes to the reality of the needs of the world. We are called to speak up. All following the light Christ shines on the world.

We are called to listen to the sound of Christ's voice.

John tells us the man born blind speaks and the Pharisees say they don't hear him. He is speaking, but they hear nothing. The Pharisees missed it, but the man born blind could hear what Jesus was offering. So, the man needles the Pharisees, he speaks up and challenges them, asking if they'd like to hear him tell the story again so that perhaps they could be Jesus' disciples. They are furious.

The Pharisees were more focused whether Jesus was healing on the Sabbath than on the compassion of recognizing the miracle that a man who had been blind could now see. If someone had a different religious view of them, they rejected the person as a sinner.

Too often we are quick to condemn those who think differently than we do.

We have to listen.

In a world of sound bites and talk radio, of divisions and riots, or prejudices and assumptions, some of the most important work the church can contribute is to listen. Training ourselves to listen to each other. And to the pain and needs of the world.

The Pharisees were spiritually blind. They refused to listen. They spoke in prejudice and accusations rather than grace. They saw nothing, heard nothing, spoke nothing helpful.

Our lesson tells us that Jesus shined a light on the man born blind and he who once was lost, was now found. He was blind, but now he sees. Physically and spiritually.

Christian Followership

Christ too can open our eyes like with the blind man, and help us realize that being spirituality alive, awake, and attentive is more important than any physical or other limitation we have or face.

That we might also seek not to condemn people but give them a second chance. That we might open our senses to the Spirit. To speak up for others. To listen to hear what others are saying. That we might listen for Christ's call.

God continues to speak to us through Jesus Christ, God's Word made flesh, the Word for us, in his example and message, his calling and caring, his love for creation, his light in our lives. In our time, he speaks and seeks to open our eyes that we may see the needs of the world and the humanity of all.

That we might open our ears to hear the cries for help and to listen to each other. That we may open our mouths and speak up in the time we live, rather than seeing no evil, hearing no evil, and speaking no evil. To open our mouths to speak the truth, to support, and to sing his praises. He calls us, in a word, to be his disciples. May it be so. Amen.

Let us pray. *Loving God help us to open our eyes, to hear your voice and to speak love to the world. Amen.*

John 10

God is like a shepherd to his disciples, to us. And if we listen for God's voice, eventually it will lead us back to God. Especially when we feel lost.

Maybe the most beloved image of the relationship between Christians, humans, people, and God, is that of our being sheep, who follow our shepherd. It's a simple comparison. One which people throughout history, throughout the world, can relate to. Recently, families at our church watched the movie Zootopia (Disney, 2016). It's a great film. In it the villain is, surprisingly, a sheep named Bellwether. The surprise only works because we expect the sheep to be good. We do so, in part because we love the image of people and their relationship with God being like a sheep with a shepherd.

We find it helpful in part because of the 23rd Psalm. Perhaps the most beloved line of the Bible comes from it. "The Lord is my shepherd. I shall not want. He maketh me lie down in green pastors. He leadeth me beside the still waters. He restoreth my soul."

I love that scripture. I said it over my children night after night for years. I have said it lying on a hospital floor caring for a loved one. I have said it in times of peril. I know because I have been with many people when they said it, that we cling to it too. We do so because we humans instinctively believe that the shepherd is dedicated to us. That is why we look to the Psalm 23 when we are in trouble. Because the shepherd is good and is dedicated to us.

John 10 tells us that Jesus uses this metaphor. It is one of Jesus's I am statements. He says, "I am the good shepherd." The shepherd who helps find the sheep when they are lost. He uses a metaphor that was frequently used by the prophets of Israel. It was said Moses was selected to be the shepherd of Israel in part because he helped save a lamb which had been lost. King David was originally a shepherd. Jesus was a prophet. He was called the new Moses. Jesus was in the line of David.

Jesus is indeed our good shepherd who is dedicated to us. The shepherd knows us. He protects us. He gives us abundance. He is dedicated to his disciples.

Why do we think the shepherd is dedicated to us? Because, as Jesus tells us, the shepherd both knows us and cares for us. The shepherd knows our name. Knows everything about it. And loves us. The shepherd knows each sheep by name. It is in connection with them, even communion with them. The shepherd is concerned about the welfare, growth, and general well-being of each individual sheep. He is concerned about your welfare too. The shepherd is concerned about each member of the flock. He knows each of us by name.

The shepherd knows each sheep's name, history, and challenges. Too often in our culture we hide our weaknesses. Thus, we hide our true selves. For we fear that if someone truly knows us, they'll never love us.

The Apostle Peter suggests that we humans have a multitude of shortcomings.

When one of gets married, one knows another human being so well that they learn well the faults of another person. If we abide in God's love, we can overcome them. For God's love covers our multitude of faults. So, a couple can be authentic with each other and trust each other with their shortcomings. Knowing each other and caring for each other.

Jesus says the shepherd knows the sheep. He says, "I am the good shepherd. I know my own and my own know me." That he knows their names. In a pastoral sense, the shepherd spends so much time that the shepherd grows to know the movements and habits and sounds of each individual sheep. We are Jesus' sheep. Jesus knows us so well as to know our sins and faults and shortcomings. The shepherd knows us. And cares for us. He loves us. In Christ, in grace, our good shepherd forgives our sins and sets up free from them.

The shepherd is dedicated to us in that the shepherd protects us. One of the roles of the shepherd was to protect or defend the sheep. In Palestine at the time, sheep were kept for wool and not for meat. The shepherd protects us from the bandits or thieves or from being lost in this challenging world.

They might be attacked by wild animals. The shepherd would protect them.

The shepherd does not jump on the wall or over the gate where the sheep gather for the night. The shepherd entered through the gate or the door. The shepherd has authority to help enter the door.

The shepherd's dedication to the sheep was so complete that as Jesus says, he would lay down his life for the sheep.

Shepherds care for the sheep. They would find them when they are lost.

I was heading home from sports practice earlier this year with one of our sons driving on Bradley Blvd about a mile south of the church when we passed a friend running down Bradley in the opposite direction chasing a dog. Calling after it. My friend calling the dog's name over and over. So, I dropped off our kids and circled back to try and help our neighbor find their dog. I called into two of my church lay ministry meetings helping to circle around trying to find the dog. Lay ministry meetings are in the evening of course so this was after dark and thus especially hard to find the lost animal.

Jesus suggests in this metaphor the idea of the shepherd who would sleep at the gate or door of the area where they sheep were laying down. He would sleep at the threshold of the door so that no predator could get in. Thus, the shepherd became a kind of living door to protect the sheep.

At one point I found my neighbor and learned that their front door had gotten open and our friend hadn't attended the door and the dog had run off.

The owner was running down our road around 7:30pm so after dark. That was kind of dangerous, that was a sacrifice. The hired hand only cares for their own safety. Not the shepherd. But while we were at the light on Bradley and Wilson and our neighbor ran past, I could see the look on our neighbor's face, that they were quite scared for the animal. That they cared very much about the animal and wanted to ensure no harm came to it. He was dedicated to it. We joined them in sending an email to the wider neighbors that the dog had been lost.

I know that this friend had just gotten a new rescue dog and the neighbor chasing it was not the neighbor who usually cared for it. So, the dog wasn't used to its new home. It was a new dog so didn't know his voice. This was the parents who didn't spend as much time caring for the animal. Jesus says the sheep will not follow a stranger, but they will run from him because they do not know his voice. That is what happened here. The animal didn't recognize the voice calling to it on Bradley Blvd. so kept running.

But over time the good shepherd pursues us with dedication and finally we recognize the voice of our good shepherd and we return home.

The good shepherd cares about the sheep. Seeks to keep them sane. Follows us when we are lost. Stands at the gate of life to ensure we don't get lost or nothing gets into harm us. The good shepherd is willing to go to great lengths to protect the sheep, to sacrifice for them, even lay down its life them.

The sheep can trust the shepherd. The very next section of John's gospel tells of the Festival of Dedication. Also known as Hanukah. The rededication of the temple. Where the shepherd is so dedicated to the sheep that he brings them eternal life. The ultimate protection. It is through the death of this particular shepherd that we as his followers are raised to new life.

Jesus tells us the shepherd gives abundance. He says, "I came that they may have life, and have it abundantly." Jesus is the shepherd who gives abundant life. He gives life abundance. Not limited life, but abundant life to the flock.

The flock here is often considered to be the church. The church represents God's abundance. Abundant blessings, abundant gratitude, abundant giving. This is what Dedication Sunday celebrates. That we need to be dedicated to the shepherd as he is dedicated to us. Dedicated to the church. Commit to God and dedicate ourselves and our resources.

Abundance also means diversity. Jesus closes this section pointing out that "I have other sheep that do not belong to this fold." This is true. There were sheep that were not of Jesus' original flock. This harkens to the idea that the great debate in the early church was whether Christianity was going to be a faith for one ethnicity or whether it would be multiethnic or multi-racial. Whether only Jews could be part of the flock. Jesus was Jewish, would his flock be made up only of people from his group or would it be multi-ethnic. Jesus chooses diversity, saying he "must bring these others also." Much like Paul would choose diversity. Much like the early church would choose diversity in welcoming gentiles. Jesus says there are sheep which are not from my fold. Part of the abundant life of Jesus includes diversity.

Abundance doesn't just mean the absence of danger; it means a more meaningful life. This is a hard time of life, a hard year. You may feel this year has been dull and difficult and we are compressed and constrained. Many of us feel lost.

Verse 9 describes the security of being able to come and in and out of our homes safely. Many of us don't during this time. This is a time with Covid when many of us have felt afraid to leave our homes. Not everyone in America feels safe with our police in our day. Many of us don't feel secure in our world.

There is an old phrase that "if the shepherd is not fed, the sheep get eaten." This applies to the sheep as well. We must be fed. We must take care of ourselves before we can take care of others.

Many of us feel lost now. We hurt now. We need a good shepherd. That is what the shepherd offers us. Abundant life. Especially when we feel lost.

At the end of the evening two weeks ago, our friend shared that they got a call that amazingly around 8pm in the dark, someone in another neighborhood saw the dog walking on burning Tree Road here past our church. So, our neighbors quickly drove to Burning Tree Road just passed the church. And, in their headlights, they, the other parent saw their dog walking around. The dog had run on Bradley Blvd several miles from home on Bradley Blvd. in the dark.

It hadn't recognized one parent's voice, but did the one who had cared for it. Even though it was new to this family, it did recognize the owner's voice, and jumped right back in the car and was safe. The animal responded to the dedication that had been shown in the past. It followed her because it recognized their voice. It heard the calming voice and run back into car.

Jesus compares his disciples to animals for a reason. Animals can get lost. They scare easily. Sheep get lost even more than dogs. We get lost as disciples. Yet we are Christ's sheep. He is our shepherd. During this unusual, challenging time, we hear the calming voice of our shepherd and we are called to run back to find shelter from the storm too.

We got lost this year. We are running but unsure of our destination. We are in the dark. Yet we listen for the shepherd's voice to lead us home.

We are called to respond to our shepherd's voice. The voice we hear in scripture, in prayers, in spirit. We respond by returning to the shepherd when we feel lost or hurting this year. When we hear the voice and run back to him. We respond to Christ's voice, to Christ's dedication to us by being dedicated to our shepherd. By returning to his loving arms in trust and love and commitment.

By supporting Christ's church here on earth. By investing in the kingdom of God here. By pledging to help the community.

We respond by being Jesus disciple. A sheep. By being dedicated to our shepherd.

Being dedicated to the shepherd means being a disciple of the shepherd. We don't find holiness by being in a place, but in being disciples. Even if we are out of our neighborhood on a strange street or out of our sanctuary in a strange time of social distancing we are called to respond to the shepherd.

This is part of what discipleship means. That we find holiness not in a place this time of year, but in a person. Our savior. The good shepherd. We don't dwell here. He dwells in us.

There is one shepherd. But from that one shepherd comes abundance. Abundance is costly. For the abundant life we have comes from the abundant generosity of a God so dedicated to our well-being that God is willing to go to death about back for us. So that his son, our good shepherd, might supply our need.

If you feel lost, let the good shepherd lead you. That shepherd gives you a chance to come home, for he leads us there. Jesus tells us that the shepherd not only calls us by name but leads us out. The Lord is our shepherd. We shall not want. He makes us lie down in green pastors. He leads us besides still waters. He leads us. He leads us in the restoration of our souls. He leads us in paths of righteousness for his name's sake.

Jesus suggests in verses 14 and 15 than in knowing him we know God. That the good shepherd leads us to the father.

Let the good shepherd lead you to abundance. Let the shepherd lead you to God. Lead you to safety. Lead you to holiness. Lead you home. Lead you to discipleship. Lead you to dedicate yourself to him, the good shepherd and all he stands for, for he is dedicated to you.

Let us pray. *Loving God, we hear about the importance of our dedication to God because of God's dedication to us. Help us to respond in kind. So that your son, our good shepherd, might supply our need. Amen.*

John 11

The gift to Christ's disciples. The great gift of discipleship, is that we trust in Christ. We die in Christ. We will rise with Christ as well.

There are three sections to the famous Lazarus story in John's Gospel - the illness and death of Lazarus, Jesus' reaction, and preparation to raise Lazarus, and then Jesus raising him. In it, we experience the great hope for all the saints and for us.

This passage of scripture is wonderful and beautiful in part because in it we see the full divinity and the full humanity of Jesus. There is perhaps nowhere, beyond the resurrection, where Jesus seems more divine than in raising Lazarus, and nowhere in scripture where he is more human than in weeping for him.

Jesus had a dual nature. Fully human and fully God.

The individual character of Thomas' life lifts up a number of dualities as well. Like most Jews at the time, he had two names - Thomas and Didymus. His name itself literally meant, "The twin."

In John 11, Thomas lifts two ideas in the famous Lazarus story. Thomas suggests to his fellow disciples that they go with Jesus to see Lazarus, who has died, so they could "die with him."

There is a duality of potential ideas. Did he mean go and die with Lazarus? Perhaps, but the context of what comes before, that Jesus was almost stoned in Judea, makes it seem that Thomas is suggesting they go die with Jesus. They knew that if they went with Jesus back into Judea, into Jerusalem, to see Lazarus, they might well be captured and killed. But Thomas was willing to go. This was the same Thomas who would later demand proof of Jesus' resurrection. We see no doubting Thomas here, but a devoted Thomas. Really, this is a both – and situation. For Lazarus believed in Jesus. So, if they died with Lazarus, they would also die with Christ and rise with Christ too. The deeper meaning is they would die with Jesus and rise.

We have cried together over the years in hospital waiting rooms. We have cried over the loss of jobs. And pets. And this year so many things have been lost that many of us have cried. We are in a time of grief. Some of us seem to be moving through it and its temporary. For others, grief is a constant companion.

Jesus knew grief. Jesus knew what it was like to have friend die. He was fully human as well as divine. One interesting question – Jesus knew he would raise Lazarus. So why did he cry around Lazarus' death? I think this underscores Jesus' compassion. He wept for his friend whom he loved. He wept for Mary and Martha for their sadness. He wept for all humanity as we are mortal. This shows the full empathy and compassion of Jesus.

John tells us that Jesus wept. But also, he shares with us, that weeping is not the end of the story.

I have had several friends die around the Covid time. I have been part of several memorial services in person and over zoom. There has been grief, and tears, but also light moments too.

At one service, there was one speaker who forgot his notes, he even went to his car in the middle of the service to find them but to no avail, but still gave a great eulogy.

At a memorial service of one of our long time members at our church the family talked about how our member and her future husband were at odds when one of them, but only one, was chosen to be an usher at the premiere of the film Gone with the Wind in Atlanta while the other wasn't.

A friend died unexpectedly recently too. At his service, his sister talked about how he, a very academic and not particularly stylish person, never wore a watch. Until one day he returned home to their Nebraska farm wearing a watch. His sister asked him where he got it. He said he was in New York City at a store looking at watches through a case when a striking woman came up and stood next to him and said, "That watch would look great on you." Later he asked the clerk who that strikingly beautiful women was. The clerk said it was the singer, Diana Ross. So he bought the watch. There is always sadness as we acknowledge the reality of death. But there can be humor too.

Yet when the humor fades, we need help. What helps the most, what allows us to move forward, is our faith in the power of Jesus Christ. For what he did for Lazarus he will do for us in the end. The name

Lazarus means "God helps." Indeed, in Christ, God helped Lazarus and helps all of us. This gives us hope.

What provides help, is that Christ gives hope. The hope for Lazarus. The reason he will rise again. The reason he will be restored. The hope for all the saints. The hope for reunion with those who died. The hope for us is captured in Jesus' statement, "I am the resurrection and the life. Those who believe in me, even though they die, will live." Jesus' most dramatic of his I am statements is this - "I am the resurrection and the life."

This is also the heart. This is the heart of our faith. That is the statement over our columbarium at my church. That is the heart of the faith in which many of us who have entrusted a loved one to our columbarium.

It's why Apostle Paul wrote about dying and rising with Christ in Romans 6. He wrote to Timothy, "If we have died with him, we will also live with him."

It is the deeper meaning of Thomas' statement "die with him." That whoever dies with him, whoever dies with Christ, whoever dies with faith in Jesus, will find eternal life.

Not that we won't get sick and die in this life. Acts tells us that Jesus' followers got sick. Later we learn that Lazarus dies.

But we have a new relationship with God, with ourselves, with life, when we know God has power over death. That is the promise of this part of scripture.

This is a gift to Christ's disciples. The great gift of discipleship. That we trust in Christ. We die in Christ. We will rise with Christ as well.

Jesus says to us what he says to all disciples, "Did I not tell you that if you believed, you would see the glory of God?" And they did. For Jesus cried with a loud voice, "Lazarus, come out!" And the dead man came out. Jesus said, "Unbind him, and let him go." And Lazarus, who had been dead, came alive. God helps. God helps us all. God's help, leads to hope and that is the heart of our faith.

What provides help is that Christ gives us hope. That is the heart of our faith.

Another friend died recently. He had fought cancer for years, but he knew in August of that year that he was dying.

He was done fighting. He was ready to be freed. He wanted to die in upstate New York where I once worked for him. So, he stopped treatment, and his two brothers drove him cross country from southern California to New York where he stayed and was cared for by hospice.

I spoke with him in early October and was able to express my gratitude to him. The focus of my friend's life was peace and justice. His goal was to make it to Indigenousness' People's Day in October. That was his goal.

On a Sunday in October, a dear friend of both of ours went to be with him, who at that point hadn't really responded to anyone in days. My friend said to him, "You know, tomorrow is Indigenousness People's Day." And he responded for the first time in days by squeezing our mutual friend's hand.

He died the next morning. He was freed. Freed from fear of all those things he was struggling with this year. Freed from grief. Freed from fighting the cancer. Freed from setting goals and agendas.

Freed into something too. Freed into faith. That as he died in Christ, that as he "died with him," he would be raised with him too. Like Lazarus, he was unbound. He was freed.

What provides help, is that Christ gives hope. We weep, as Jesus did. But we have hope too. Hope for all the Saints and for us.

That we will be freed someday. Freed from fear of all those things we are grieving. Freed from fighting. Freed from setting agendas.

Freed into faith too. Freed into Christ. That as we die in Christ, that as we "die with him," we will be raised with Christ too. Unbound and able to finally see the glory of God. May it be so.

Let us pray. *Loving God, give us the gift of faith, that we might know in our hearts that when we die with Christ, we will rise with him too. Amen.*

John 12

John 12: 25 tells us, "Those who love their life lose it, and those who hate their life in this world will keep it for eternal life." This idea is one of the keys to discipleship. More than that, it is key to a meaningful life.

Covid has been a cross to bear. Physically, financially, emotionally, spiritually.

Yet we are not alone. God is with us on the journey. The light is coming on this year. We can pick up our cross and follow Jesus. We can find meaning yet.

The story has often been told of an Italian priest suffering from Covid named Don Berardelli who gave up his ventilator so another person could live. Berardelli was suffering so his parish bought him a ventilator. But at a time when many in Italy were suffering from lack of ventilators, the 72-year-old priest gave his ventilator for a younger patient and died a year ago next week. He put the needs of another first. His sacrifice led to meaning.

There is mounting evidence that there is value to getting out of your own heads. That happiness is found in devoting oneself to causes greater than one's own self-interest, as John McCain would put it. That we find the most purposeful life in trying not to hoard, store up or focus on one's own life, but by pouring out that life into the well-being of others in the world. If you think over your life, if you are like me, you might recall that many of the most satisfying moments in most of our lives come from times when we forget ourselves, either by losing oneself in the moment or doing something for someone else.

This is what disciples do.

This is the wisdom of one of the great passages in the Bible.

Jesus makes a powerful statement. A version is included in all four Gospels. As Mark records it, Jesus says, "If you would follow me, take up your cross. If you try and save your life, you will lose it. If you lose it for my sake, you will save it." That can be hard, but it's the best way to the meaningful life Peter sought.

In Jesus' day, there was nothing sacred about a cross. It was used to torture and kill those who opposed Rome. Crosses would be all along the path to Jerusalem, with bodies on them. Crosses were meant for humiliation, torture, and deterrence, as a warning to others.

Yet Jesus redeemed it. Jesus showed that any part of life and of our world, no matter how challenging, challenged, and difficult for us, could be remade into an instrument of life. And that when we are willing to think of the well-being of others, to get outside our own heads for a moment, with God's help we are able redeem our lives and our own corner of the world.

Now to be clear, to accept Jesus' invitation to take up our cross does not mean subjugating ourselves so that we accept abuse or seeing ourselves as any less than God made us to be. Instead it means to live authentically. To follow him is an invitation to join him in treating others with dignity, pushing back at division, and living our lives in such a way that we affirm others and find meaning in what we give. To find our meaning outside ourselves. To invest in our relationships outside ourselves. To find meaning in discipleship, in following the one who leads us to the meaningful life we seek.

Jesus not only says pick up our cross, he says "whoever will lose their life will gain it." This is what Jesus offered.

The black plague of the 15th and 16th centuries had immediate and long ranging impacts. It also impacted the Protestant Reformers and the church in profound ways.

This scripture from Mark 8 influenced John Calvin to write in his Institutes that "We are not our own....We belong to the Lord. Therefore, let us live and die to and for the Lord."

This is what Martin Luther did. Medieval Europe was ravaged by the Bubonic Plague when at least twenty-five percent of its population was lost. The fifteenth century also witnessed related epidemics. Several times, people implored Luther to leave his town and try and flee the epidemic, but he refused to leave. He stayed to help those who suffered. He lost two children to the disease. He felt compelled to pick up his cross and follow Jesus.

Whoever loses their live will save it. John 10 tells us Jesus said, "A good shepherd lays down his life for the sheep, but the hired hand sees the wolf coming and flees." And John later says, there is no greater love than to lay down one's live for their friends.

I'm currently reading a biography of Dietrick Bonhoeffer (Eric Metaxas, Bonhoeffer: Pastor, Martyr, Prophet, Spy, Thomas Nelson Publishers, 2011). Dietrich Bonhoeffer was a German pastor and executed during World War II by the Nazis. He knew wrote about how giving of oneself in following Jesus has a price, but the reward is like nothing else. He called it the "cost of discipleship." In 1939, just before the war, Bonhoeffer was in New York, at Union Seminary. Friends told him not to return to Germany where things had gotten so bad. But in June of 1939, he wrote a letter to his friend, Reinhold Niebuhr, "I have had time to think and pray about my situation and that of my nation. I have come to the conclusion that… I must live through the difficult period of our national history with the Christian people of Germany….". . . And so, he boarded one of the last ships to sail from the United States to Germany, spoke out against Nazism, organized a seminary to train pastors for a prophetic ministry, and he joined the resistance and a plot to assassinate Hitler. He was arrested and was executed on April 9, 1945.

Jesus said, "If any want to become my followers, let them deny themselves and take up their cross and follow me. For those who want to save their life will lose it, and those who lose their life for my sake, and for the sake of the gospel, will find it, or save it." Save their life.

The word used in Greek for Jesus' statement about life is not bios or physical life. But something deeper. Its psyche, from where we get the word psychology. It means soul-life. We give of our lives and we get something deeper. Something soulful. Something meaningful. Our souls, the holy part within us, is the part more like God than our physical being. When we get out of ourselves and act with sacrificial love, we are most like Jesus, most like God. In doing so we find meaning and purpose and we might even discover joy.

I have a good friend who I have shared conversations and ministries over the years, who wrote me recently that they weren't feeling well. Feeling down. And alone. Thinking about where they could find meaning in life. Asking, "What is this life all about? Is it worth it?" Medication didn't help. In fact, it only made the person feel worse.

My friend had been praying for purpose for a while. They shared that their daily prayer became "God, please help me. Give me something important to do, something that will make me feel I matter . . . to someone! I will do my best to take it on. All I want is a chance." Still, nothing happened right away.

Then one day on a bus ride, they found themselves sitting across a person who was talking about starting a housecleaning business. The two individuals talked. They were different backgrounds, races, genders, economic experiences, but made a connection.

My friend was thinking about having their home cleaned, so they gave the person their card and suggested perhaps the person call when they had time and come over the clean.

The person came over to my friend's house and shared about their life. About tragically losing their son. About their dream of starting a business. They didn't have much experience with business and all the rules and regulations and taxes, so my friend began to work with the person on setting up and helping the person with their business. My friend shared too, shared time and expertise. Helping with accounting. Referring clients.

Later, when the person's housing situation turned out to be a dangerous, my friend helped the person find a new place to live. So, they arranged for the person to stay at a local hotel, where the management was so impressed, they want the person to join their cleaning staff.

My friend felt valued and needed. In reflecting on what getting outside themselves and helping meant, my friend wrote, "I truly believe God connected us. I already knew that God answers prayers, but at my lowest, when I asked, the answers came. I will say, I realize that the problems I face have not gone away. But they feel less important now...I think I am now prepared if they come back. I know God will be with me. I may find suffering, like we all eventually will do, but I know I will find support when I need it. God loves us all."

We all face suffering. Even Jesus did. Jesus had to convince Peter that suffering is part of this life, even for him. But the key to a meaningful life is not to stay focused solely on oneself and what one gains and losses. To pick up our cross and follow Jesus. As Peter eventually did. To pour out of lives to help others. To save and find our soulful meaning in life.

Like a mother giving all to an infant. A grown child helping a parent in transition. A neighbor driving a friend to a vaccine appointment. A person working long hours on a cause. A Christian picking up their cross and following Jesus, all the way to Holy Week. For in that we find our meaning in life.

The 19th century English philosopher John Stuart Mill wrote "those only are happy who have their minds fixed on some object other than their own happiness; on the happiness of others, on the improvement of (human) kind."

The past year has reminded us that we have one life to live. Jesus makes clear in our scripture that life is most alive when we get outside ourselves and help.

We hear one of the most powerful invitations of Jesus. To pick up our cross and follow him. A call to discipleship. For John 12: 25 tells us, "Those who love their life lose it, and those who hate their life in this world will keep it for eternal life."

For those who try to save their life will lose it, and those who lose their life for his sake, and for the sake of the gospel, will find their life. We hear the invitation. How will we respond?

Let us pray. *Loving God, help us to feel your presence, your calling and to have the courage to respond. We long to find more meaning in life. Help us to find it in you. Amen.*

John 13

John 13: 34-35 tells us Jesus said,

"A new command I give you: Love one another. As I have loved you, so you must love one another. By this everyone will know that you are my disciples, if you love one another."

This is a scripture that inspires a section of John's Gospel that flows through John 17, that can inspire us to choose love in our world.

John 13 begins the farewell discourses of Jesus, where he instructs his disciples as he moves towards his passion. He gives them a commandment to love one another. So that people will know they are his disciples.

One fascinating study recently focused on the increasing propensity of each side of America's political divide to view the other as less than human.

This is where the church can help. For the church, with all its flaws and own divisions, has been effective in promoting a theology that everyone is made in the image of God. That we reflect the image of God the most when we love. And that everyone in the world is entitled and deserving of love.

John emphasizes over and over again that Jesus talked about love.

Love, agape, serves as the frame for the whole chapter. We hear about this love in the beginning, that he "loved his own who were in the world."

John 3 says that God so loved the world that God gave God's only son.

We often read John 13 on Maundy Thursday. That Jesus gives us a new commandment to love one another. In fact, Jesus went beyond this and said that,

"By this everyone will know that you are my disciples, if you have love for one another." Here we hear for first time of Jesus' love for his disciples. Disciples are those who recognize Jesus as one with God. That the words and actions of Jesus are the words and actions of God and so they endeavor to follow them. And that part of our calling as disciples is to love one another.

John 14 and 15 and over and over John talked about love. That love is the most central aspect of the character of God.

And then in John 17, we hear "I made your name known to them…. so that the love with which you have loved me may be in them, and I in them." To know a name is to know something personally. To know the name of God is to know God personally.

It's a prayer, near the end of his meal with his disciples, near the end of his life, when Jesus prayed for unity of his people. This is part of the longest, and in some ways the most personal, prayer Jesus prays that we have record of. The great reformer Philip Melanchthon wrote that there were no words on heaven or earth more holy than Jesus' prayer here. It's said that Scottish reformer John Knox had this prayer read to him over and over on his deathbed. In the portion we read from today, Jesus prays as he places the community's future in God's hands. These are words to God in prayer but have great implications for the communities of all who would be Jesus' disciples.

He prayed that we might be one. Much as Jesus is connected so deeply with God, revealing the glory of God, that the world would be blessed through Jesus' disciples. When we disciples know God loves us, it makes us easier for us to put aside our differences and find healing, unity, and love. And perhaps to inspire unity in our divide world.

It is so the love and spirit of Jesus is in us. When we realize that God's love is in Jesus, that Jesus is in us, that connects us with God. We are not just individual people out on our own. We are made in the image of God. We all, all of us, are loved by God. So is our neighbor. Our opponent. The person with whom we disagree. That can lead to love. When we love we reflect the character and heart of God, that can lead to unity.

In John 17, the third and final section of Jesus' prayer, Jesus is not praying only for his disciples. He is praying for the world. The others. The people outside his immediate flock. That others outside his following might be blessed through them. He is praying for everyone. That all may come and know God. That all might be blessed. That all are deserving of love. So, by loving one another, Jesus means first the disciples. But he doesn't mean just other disciples. He means people outside one's own current small group, beyond those who think like us now, beyond those who are like us – everyone.

During another divided period, his political opponents, the Pharisees, asked Jesus a question intended not for honest feedback, but political points. Matthew tells us that Jesus asked by Pharisees in Matthew 22 what was the greatest commandment. In this question the Pharisee were trying to get Jesus by asking him what the greatest commandments was. They were trying to catch him in a verbal trap. Scripture tells us they were trying to test him. Or trap him as some would say.

The Pharisees had tried to trap Jesus before with someone easy questions. But this is this serious question. Which is greatest commandment from God. They no doubt schemed to catch Jesus in a careless statement so they could condemn him for heresy or brand him as a radical.

Jesus didn't let them trap him. Jesus responded by love. But Jesus passed the test. Jesus answered consistent with the Hebrew Bible. He answered with love.

In John 13, Jesus tells us to love one another.

Love will get us through too. No matter who we disagree with if we disagree in love we can get through. No matter who we voted for if we look to love we can get through. If we are to be the church, to be disciples, we must lead with and model love to a world which needs it. This is a time of great disappointment for some of us. And a time of great anxiety. We must be willing and able to hear perspectives that differ from our own, so we don't end up at the extremes.

We also ought to love the people around us. Not only a few of them, not just the people who agree with us or are on our side or seem easy to love. We are called to love one another. Period. Without exception.

I officiated a wedding of two church members recently at Sugarloaf Mountain. A great couple. In their vows I could feel the depth of their love. We talked in the homily about how there will be of course times when they, like every couple, disagree. But love will get them through too, for it flows from God's love for us.

Jesus emphasizes in his scripture that we not only belong to God; we belong to each other. We are to love one another, as God loves us. That we have unity because God's love is in Jesus and Jesus is in us. That the greatest commandments are linked. We love God and love one another. We are called to follow this commandment.

The first half of John's Gospel describes eternal life as the fruit of relationships with God. Yet in this second half, we hear that a relationship of love, love with God and with each other, becomes the gift from God. That the world's unity should mirror the unity of God and Jesus. There is unity with God and Jesus. There should be unity with Jesus and disciples. There should be unity among the disciples. And there should be unity with those people outside the disciples' comfort zone. By loving one another, Jesus doesn't mean just other disciples. He means people outside one's own current small group, beyond those who think like us now, beyond those who are like us – everyone.

In the last part of Jesus' prayer, Jesus expands his focus from the community of believers to the broader world, and how the world is, in all its division, might be positively impacted, even healed, by the covenant community. He prays for the broader community outside his own.

Churches can be divided too. I had a pastor at a church I used to serve quip that the main spiritual gift of some members of the church was litigation.

Mother Theresa put it this way, "If we have no peace it's because we have forgotten we belong to each other."

If we are anxious during this time. If you are in a challenging time with this Covid or anything else, lean on your church. Let's find a time to talk. Lean on each other. We belong to each other.

Much as churches will not worship God the same way, people in the world will not believe the same things, yet the love of God can transcend differences. It may be the only thing capable of breaking down barriers and bringing real unity.

In a nation, even a world, where there are too many barriers and walls, we are the church. And the church at its best says that in the kingdom of God there are no walls or barriers here.

Jesus makes his announcements we read of around his last Supper. There are no walls of race, gender, orientation, party affiliation, ideology, around this round table in particular, this table, a symbol that has no sharp edges, reminds us that all are welcome at the table of Christ. Not because we are worthy but because we are welcome by God's grace. At the table we say the gifts of God given for all because God loves each of us. And we should love each other in return.

God's love receives us, accepts us, completely as we are—with all our faults—and is a love that doesn't just leave us where we are, but calls forth our own love in response. A love that we cannot ever earn or deserve but a love that is for us, is in us, never leaves us, and challenges us not to like everyone necessarily, but to love them.

According to John, this prayer would be the final time Jesus addressed his disciples as a group. This part of scripture is the entrance to Jesus' passion, as God's love in the world is poured out in the passion of Christ, creating beloved community here. This section speaks of Christ's work. His work was to complete the calling of God to go, as chapters 18 and 19 tell us, and sacrifice for the world. God so loved the world that God gave God's only son.

Christ's work was to go into a world that was divided and difficult and hostile and pay the price for us in that world. The world will know we are his disciples, that is those who follow Christ even when it's difficult, if we do the difficult work of loving the world, including those who oppose us or are difficult or who seem to be on the other side. This is where unity is found. Where glory is experienced. This is how the world becomes one. The work of the disciples was to live with Christ in them, Christ working through them, to show Christ's love to the world. For in the kingdom of God there is unity of the Father and the son, and so there should be unity within the human family.

We are called by God to return love. But by returning it, I don't mean that we pay God back by loving God back. We mortals are not capable of paying God back by loving God as God as loved us. Instead, God wants us to pay it forward, by loving each other. Loving each and every one.

Martin Luther King Jr. had a gift of being able to love people, even when they hated him. I love how King put it, "I have decided to stick with love. Hate is too great a burden to bear." When we choose hate, we soon find ourselves alone, by ourselves, focused on our own needs, bearing the burden of emotion solo. Yet when we choose love, Christ is in us. God's love is in us. Jesus carries us. We are not alone.

Only love, love for God and for one another can transform our lives, our nation, our world. As we seek healing as we worship after a national election, may we seek love, for love can bring healing.

In March of 1861, with the nation on the cusp of a civil war that would begin six weeks later, Abraham Lincoln stood on the steps of the capitol and delivered his first inaugural address. Lincoln, whose Christian faith included his decisions and his speech, appealed to God in his address for help. But he also appealed to his countrymen for unity.

Lincoln closed his address with these words, "We are not enemies, but friends. We must not be enemies. Though passion may have strained, it must not break our bonds of affection. The mystic chords of memory, stretching from every battlefield and patriot grave to every living heart and hearthstone all over this broad land, will yet swell the chorus of the Union, when again touched, as surely they will be, by the better angels of our nature."

Friends, as we as we seek to choose, discover, and find unity rather than division at this critical time, let us choose love. For our land, our nation, our country, at this critical time, may the spirit of love, the better angels of our nature, prevail.

May God's grace make it so.

Let us pray. *Loving God, in all our challenges and all our gifts, help us to choose love. In the midst of this challenging time, hay your spirit connect us and make us one. In gratitude to you and for the wellbeing of ourselves and our world. Amen.*

John 14

As Jesus' disciples we follow a God who, in Christ, is always and forever our "home."

You likely have heard the phrase that "home is where the heart is." Some say it came from a 1829 poem, "'Tis home where the heart is," in The Fayetteville Weekly Observer. Elvis Pressley helped make the phrase famous by singing it in 1961 film Kid Galahad, "Home is where the heart is, and my heart is anywhere you are. Anywhere you are is home."

This is a time in history when we are at home, during the pandemic. Where we have been working from home, with kids doing school from home.

The Biblical expression of where God dwells in our tradition progresses over time to be closer and closer to us.

Originally, God's people viewed God as being only in the Heavens. 3000 years ago, the Israelites believed that God's presence was rooted in the Temple in Jerusalem. That if one wasn't in the Temple, near the holiest of holies, one wasn't near God. But then after the destruction of the Temple and then the Israelites exile away from Jerusalem to Babylon, the focus shifted towards synagogues.

When Jesus arrived the theology of the incarnation focused on a God who wasn't just far away in the heavens, but willing to come to be with us here near to us, personally and individually.

Then as John tells it, when Jesus began to prepare for his departure from earth, to return to his heavenly home, he promised the Holy Spirit would come and be even closer to people. Very personal, individual, and up close. In a later section of John 14, Jesus says that if his disciples love him the Spirit will come and abide in them.

When scripture details God's dwelling place, it often relates to love. When we read that we will dwell in the house of the Lord forever, Psalm 23 uses the image of a shepherd who loves his flock. In Revelation 21, where we read that God's house is among the mortals, we hear of the image of a bride and husband on their wedding day. And in John 14, where Jesus says that in my father's house there are many dwelling places, the following sentence is where Jesus says, "Do not let your hearts be troubled."

Right before Jesus tells the disciples in John there are many rooms in his father's house, he tells them that he is leaving, and they are upset. So, he gives them a gift. A gift to help them feel close when he is gone and before they can all go to his father's house. He says, "I give you a new commandment," but it's really a gift. He says "love one another. As I have loved you, you should love one another. By this everyone will know you are my disciples if you love one another." He says this is a new commandment, but really this is a gift to return the disciples home to the love of God and neighbor found in the book of Leviticus. You see the progression, God being in the Heavens, the temple, the synagogue, the savior, the spirit and now out in love among the people.

There is a connection between hearts and God's home. Between the house of the Lord and love. That when we love one another we are most like God. We most reflect God's nature. So if we want to be near God, if we want to feel God close, if we want the spirit of Jesus near us when we feel so distant from everything else, we should remember that home is where the heart is, and find our home in God's love.

At a time when so much of our politics and culture, country and world are punctuated by division and hate, the church can do perhaps its greatest service by modeling the love of one another. By demonstrating that love is possible in and for our world.

John 14 begins with Jesus saying that in his father's house or home there are many dwelling places. This is a vision of heaven. Jesus told his disciples in his farewell discourses which began in John 13 that he was preparing to depart from this world. They are upset. They wanted to go with Jesus. He tells them that they cannot go now with him, but that someday they will be able to go to the place where he goes, for he prepares a place for them and will come back and get them. Yet Jesus's disciples wonder if they are ever going to be able to return with Jesus to be with God in the heavens. They, like the prodigal son and even King David in the Old Testament, wonder if they can ever return home. Part of Jesus' point here is that we can always return home to God in faith.

My friend Martha lives in my neighborhood. For New Year's Eve last year, her son called from L.A. to Capitol Beer and Wine on Norfolk Avenue here in Bethesda to order a bottle of champagne to be delivered to his mom. I like that store as much for their dark chocolate as their wine. They had a particular chocolate bar with fennel on it I used to love. Anyway, Martha called Capitol Beer and Wine to have it delivered. She was told that no more deliveries were going out for New Years. Her son didn't like that, so he decided to call the man back one more time saying how near to Norfolk Avenue was to his mom's house, and gave the specific address number on Honeywell Lane. Her son was asked to repeat the address, to which the proprietor said, "I will deliver it myself, free, because I am Justin and I grew up in that house on Honeywell Lane! That was my home." So, Justin came to Martha's door on New Year's Eve with the bottle of champagne and repeated the connection between him and that house he moved from 41 years ago. A place where he had felt love. The boy from whose family Martha had purchased the home 41 years ago made her delivery on New Year's Eve.

In love, we can always return home. In faith, God is a God of steadfast love. It's never too late to return home to God. Jesus' point is that he glorifies God not only through his ministry on earth, but by how Jesus works through his followers by their returning home by leaning into his love.

When Jesus prepares to return to his father's dwelling place, he does so after the grand adventure of living among us. The Word became flesh and dwelt among us. And here the Word, Jesus, returns to God.

When Jesus talks about his father's house, he shares it with his disciples, personally and individually. When Jesus talks about the vision of heaven, his father's house, he doesn't describe one big hall with lots of cots and bunk beds or lying in sleeping bags on the floor. "In his father's house there are many dwelling places, or houses or mansions," as the King James puts it. Many individual spaces. Home is both community and it's a place where each individual belongs.

It is why the prodigal son can be welcomed home in love after his adventures. It's like Max in Where the Wild Things Are, who returns home because he longs to be back in a place where he is loved best of all. Because, as Dorothy would say, after all the adventures of life, there is no place like home.

I saw humorist Ann Landers and others have lifted up a story called "The City of Our Dreams." It tells the tale of a normal man who left his village, tired of his life, hoping for someplace where he could escape all the struggles of this earth. He set out in search of a magical, special place - the heavenly city of his dreams, where all things would be perfect. He walked all day and by dusk, near the end of the day, found himself in a forest, where he decided to spend the night. Eating the bread, he had brought, he said his prayers and, just before going to sleep, placed his shoes in the center of the path, pointing them in the direction he would continue the next morning. Little did he imagine that while he slept, someone came along and turned his shoes around, pointing them back in the direction from which he had come.

The next morning, in all the new light, he got up, gave thanks to God, and started on his way again in the direction that his shoes pointed. For a second time he walked all day, and towards evening finally saw the magical city in the distance. It wasn't as large as he had expected. As he got closer, it looked curiously familiar. But he pressed on, found a street very much like his own, knocked on a familiar door, greeted the family he found there - and lived happily ever after in the city of his dreams.

This is a year of distant wonderings. Where we do school and work and life and church in new ways. Where we have been away from our church for a year on a seeming journey. And who knows exactly what things in the world will be like when we return.

The church a place that loves you. A place that has not forgotten you. A place you can feel God's love through each other. It may not be fancy. It may not be perfect. But it's where you are loved. And in that it provides a foretaste of the love we will experience someday in God's house with Jesus. For here you are loved individually and personally. A place where you are wanted and needed.

One of our church leaders wrote to me recently about their decision to be more involved with leadership of the church. The person wrote, "When I was thinking about the church, I realized "'I am home.'" I was thinking about my current being, not physical being, but rather spiritual. Our life journeys are long and arduous." Then the member wrote, "At a point in our journey, if we can feel God's unconditional (even steadfast) love and presence, I think that's when we might say "I am home."

I hope the church can be such a place for you.

When Jesus says love one another, he organizes that love around a unity of disciples, a place, a home, an institution – the church. Also known as the body of Christ.

Jesus goes to prepare a place for us in God's house, but also in his gift to God's people of a community that, at its best, is about love. Jesus invites us to join him here in his home of steadfast love.

As we walk the sometimes long and arduous journey of this life, there are places that can truly represent God to us. It is my own spiritual experience that this church is that kind of place.

A place that can help us realize that it is never too late to go home. There is no place like our spiritual home.

A place where we can use our God-given gifts and live out the gift that when we love one another as God has loved us, we grow in likeness of our Lord.

So that even if are separated, as long as we are Christ's disciples, through the church we can realize that home is where the heart is. That our hearts can be joined. So, we can feel at home in God's love. May it be so.

Let us pray. *Loving God, in the midst of this challenging time, may your spirit connect us and make us one. Amen.*

John 15

What makes discipleship most effective is when we stay connected to the vine of Jesus Christ.

Fall is a wonderful time of year for trees. Differing colors, lots of beauty. One Friday, my daughter and I camped out our backyard and, in the tent, we could hear the wind rustle through the branches overhead. We talked through a park yesterday and picked up leaves to take pictures of them to email to my mom in Ohio to ask her to identify their trees from the leaves.

We hear about branches and vines in our scripture from John 15. John 15 begins the section of final words Jesus said as he walked out of Jerusalem towards the Garden of Gethsemane near the end of his life. He might has passed by tree branches or rows of vines or a vine on a home or the ornamental vine on the temple, and it reminded him to use the idea of a vine and branches when talking with his disciples in one of his final ways of describing himself.

As we look to be the branches which bear fruit for God in our time, we consider all we have to steward for God's glory.

This Covid season is a time when there is a sense of scarcity in the world. Too few supplies. Too much social distance. Not enough connectedness. And in the face of it, we here in this church rebel against a culture of scarcity by saying that with God there is still abundance. God is bigger than Covid. With God all things are possible. God will supply our needs.

Some people say the glass is half empty, some the glass is half full. The Christian agrees with the writer of Psalm 23 that "my cup runneth over." It's easy this year to see the glass as half empty. With Covid and national division and economic challenge. But I believe the church in all its imperfect abundance is more vital than ever. Being a place of connection when Covid has forced social distancing. Being a place of spiritual sustenance and unity in a time of heartache and division. Providing help in a variety of missional ways on some of the key issues of our day.

In our scripture, Jesus says to "abide in me." What does it mean to abide?

In our culture we might think of the hymn, Abide With Me, which we sing at funerals as we allow Christ to carry us in grief. For those fans of the irreverent film The Big Lebowski, it speaks of the "Dude abiding," which implies his making it through a variety of challenges.

In John 15, Jesus uses the word abide to mean that we are to stay connected to Jesus. That we make him our support, our balance, the one we trust, much as branches are connected to a vine. The vine is connected to the roots and provides the nourishment for the branches to live. Without the vine, the branches get naturally pruned, wither and die.

So too do we. For without Jesus we lose our hope that there is something after death. Without Jesus we lose our model for abundant living now. Without Jesus our attention moves to things which don't give life.

John 15 details Jesus using a metaphor of a vine to explain how we can abide. Jesus makes the final of his famous "I am" statements in John and say, "I am the vine, the true vine, and you are the branches."

Jesus' statement is in contrast to the Hebrew Bible view of Israel as the vine of God. Israel has been described as God's vineyard in Psalms, Jeremiah, Hosea, Isaiah, and Ezekiel. The nation, the country, thought of itself as the vine. So much so that the vine became a national symbol of the kingdom of Israel. The vine was on some coins at the time, and a symbol on its temple. Some commentators have said that it was the national symbol of Israel at the time. Sort of a bald eagle of Israel.

Jesus said I, not Israel, not one's ethnic identity, not the empire, not the Roman Empire, not the government, not anything else, is the true vine.

Jesus reminded the people to simplify and focus on him. If they make him their ultimate focus, if the abiding in him, not in the comings and goings of the world, is what they relied on they would find sustenance and peace.

Much like it was in the focus on Israel, abiding in the national issues is important but if that is all you have, for many of us that may be a recipe for an anxious life. Abiding in Jesus is a recipe for an abundant life.

So, abide in your spiritual life. Take a walk. Meditate. Do yoga. Read the scriptures. Pray.

Jesus is the real vine. Stay connected to him. We get abundance from Jesus. If we abide in Jesus, he will give you peace.

Jesus says that when we abide in him, he will abide in us, and we will bear much fruit. For Christ here, good fruit are good actions. Notice Jesus doesn't command the disciples to bear fruit. Rather, he calls them to abide in him. And from that realization of the blessings of God comes gratitude, and that leads to the bearing of fruit.

To bear fruit we must be grateful people. For Jesus suggests that the fruit we bear is not due to our own independent gifts or power. Our fruit comes from God. Abundant blessings lead to abundant gratitude which yields abundant giving. We are called to act in abundance.

The Apostle Paul is in prison and he writes to the Philippians: "I thank my God every time I remember you." He chose gratitude. Jonah is in the belly of the whale and prayed to God a prayer of thanksgiving. Gratitude can be a choice.

We don't choose our blessings. But we do choose whether or not to recognize them.

God's blessings are here for us to receive. But we have to choose gratitude.

When we choose gratitude, we bear fruit by realizing we have abundant blessings from God, the vine which is the source of our blessings and sustenance, and then we have abundant generosity to share, which is the fruit our blessings.

Yet no one branch, no one person, can do it all alone, can do everything the vine needs us to do, however. All of us are needed. This is what Jesus focused on in calling people to be his disciples. He called disciples in groups.

John 15 is a wonderful passage. Jesus suggests that we are the branches, connected to the vine that is Christ, and with him we can do amazing things. Separated, we are lost. That connection includes a deep friendship with Jesus. In John 15, Jesus calls his disciples friends. That they are no longer servants but that he calls them friends. We think about our relationship with Christ and we celebrate that being a disciple is not only being a learner, it means to be Jesus' friend.

More than ever it's important to think about friendship. Friends help us deal with this time. Friendship can be a spiritual practice, a gift, a gift from God, a hopeful help during difficult times.

Friendship can be hard. My grandmother used to say that if a person had one true friend, they were fortunate.

Friendships can be hard for children and youth.

Some of us are too busy to have friends. Or we act as if relationships exist to feed our agendas. We have interests in our politics or community or church. But not real friends.

Friendships were important to God. The trinity is about mutual connection. God said it was not ideal for a person to be alone. Jesus encouraged people to be in pairs. Paul traveled in teams on his missions. The Holy Spirit bound them all together.

Ralph Waldo Emerson once said, "The only way to have a friend is to be one."

Many of us turn to Facebook for friendship. And in these times, Facebook and social media can be helpful.

Yet friendship can be more, it can be of God. It can be a spiritual practice. Friendship can be part of the church. Friendship is a gift from God.

We can have friendship with each other because we are connected in friendship to the one who creates all things.

I invite you to counter the isolation of this time. To say that physical distancing does not need to mean social distancing for you. And to seek out friendship in church and outside. God is between us when friendships form. Don't just be casual acquaintances at church, be vulnerable, engaged, open and interested in friendship enough that your souls are bound together. Find holiness in friendship.

We have seen communities coming together this year dealing with covid and wildfires and economic burden.

And we have seen the negative impact when selfishness drives a person's basic decision making.

Fellow travelers are critical to us at this time. Friends will get us through this time.

Our faith can teach us about friendship. Jesus shook up his culture through relationships of love, not power and intimidation. He didn't come bullying as many political, military and even religious authorities of the day did, but he made friends by being a friend.

Jesus was interested in friendship. He was also interested in his disciples' spiritual and personal growth. Jesus didn't just want them to be blind lemmings, he wanted them to develop their own spiritual core, for he knew they would need to continue God's work after his death. I find it encouraging that Jesus was interested in the growth of those who would follow him. The key for the disciples, as the branches of God, was to remain rooted in the vine that was their Lord even as they grew. Especially as they grew.

In his Saturday Night Live (NBC) opening in March 2020, John Mulaney quipped, "I think the greatest miracle of Jesus, what is amazing about Jesus is he has 12 best friends in his thirties, and they weren't his wife's best friends' husbands… Remember when your dad went fishing once? These guys went fishing every day! And they were all best friends and he'd do magic tricks for them and they loved it." Maybe we should be move like Jesus.

Jesus cared about friends. John 15 speaks to this. He called his disciples friends. John tells us Jesus said, "I no longer call you servants, but I call you friends. For I have made known everything God has made known to me." What is amazing about Jesus is the wants us to be his friends. Jesus invites people like us, imperfect people like you and me, to be his friends.

We cannot manufacture friendship on our own. It takes two. But we can open ourselves to friendship. We can be open to being a friend, to being nice to people we've met, to being hospitable. To reach out during this covid time. To care for another, taking time for the other, listening to others, being attentive to the wants and needs of others.

Friends keep us strong. They remind us that we are not alone. That we face the challenge of life together. As the branches of God, we do well to stay rooted in the vine that is Jesus Christ and to remember what Christ teaches.

Jesus calls his disciples friends because he has made known to them everything God has made known through him. That is why every deep friendship we have is a gift from God. It's why the church seeks to encourage real friendships. Why friendship with each other reflects the loving heart of God.

So, invest in friendship. Following a savior who came to show that our God cares deeply about relationships. May that be a gift to you and to me. That we may feel called to go and do likewise.

We too are branches. When one looks at a tree it is hard to distinguish where one branch ends, and another begins. Branches are intertwined in vines or trees.

We disciples are not alone, but aligned. We align with each other in the church, the community, in order to be Christ's disciples. In order to do the work of ministry. We learn in community, the ideas of the collective, even in disagreement, helps prune the branches, so we bear more fruit.

To be a disciple means to be part of a community. It is not only our relationship with Christ that is life giving. It is our relationship with each other, the other branches on the vine, the other members of the community, which allows us to do things we cannot do on our own.

We all are the limbs, the branches of God's tree, branches of the true vine. We can do more together than we can apart. This is where you are needed. This church is where you are needed to be. Your commitment is needed.

For tree or vine to function well, it can't just have one branch, it must have many branches. A branch all by itself is exposed to wind and elements and animals and cannot survive like a branch connected to other branches. It is the same with the church. We support the church and the church supports us. For a branch to be connected to Christ means it is connected to his church. For a branch to be able to connect to the church means it can draw sustenance from the true vine. Without the vine and each other, we can do nothing.

This is a different theology in some ways from what Paul writes in 1 Corinthians. He writes famously of the metaphor of the church as a body. And each individual part of the body is unique. And there is great value in that. But here Jesus says that it's not the individual attributes that matter for the branches, it's their ability to align together in the community, to come together, that make people the branches of Christ. Their unity makes them his disciples. Every blessing counts. All gratitude counts. Every gift counts.

I have a friend who likes to say, "God doesn't have a mission for the church as much as God has a church to carry out Christ's mission in the world." We steward that legacy, that mission, that church.

Abundant blessings lead to abundant generosity which leads to abundant giving. As we abide in abundance, act in abundance, align in abundance, we realize we can do more together than we can apart. When we view the world from a mindset of abundance and live with generosity, we reflect the very nature of God.

We are Jesus's disciples. Staring up at the trees and the stars and the sky. Invited to receive our strength and sustenance and peace from the true vine of our savior. Called to act in a broken world through generous stewardship of our abundant blessings. Called to align with each other through the church. Wherever we are. To care about the world, this tree of faith, this collection of branches, from which we can draw meaning, mission, and the many abundant blessings of faith.

Let us pray. *Loving God, help us to be your disciples as we steward your many gifts. Help us to invest in relationships with you and each other. Amen.*

John 16

John 16 tells us that Jesus' disciples said, "Yes, now you are speaking plainly, not in any figure of speech! Now we know that you know all things, and do not need to have anyone question you; by this we believe that you came from God." Jesus answered them, "Do you now believe? The hour is coming, indeed it has come, when you will be scattered, each one to his home, and you will leave me alone. Yet I am not alone because the Father is with me. I have said this to you, so that in me you may have peace. In the world you face persecution. But take courage; I have conquered the world!"

This is a time in history when indeed we are scattered. Covid has separated and scattered us, each to our own home. Yet fortunately, as disciples we can take courage, for Jesus has conquered the world.

Discipleship means we are not our own savior. Instead we are witnesses. We point the way to Jesus. Just like John the Baptist.

John's Gospel explains that John came as a witness to the light. He came to testify concerning that light, so that through him all might believe.

John's Gospel and all the Gospels make clear that John was not the messiah, but he just pointed the way to the messiah who was coming into the world.

People mistook John to be the messiah. This is one of the interesting paradoxes of this part of the Bible. John the Baptist looked like a radical, but in some ways spoke like he was nothing special. John wore unusual clothes, had wild hair, dawned a camel skin coat and ate locusts and wild honey. He could have claimed all the attention, but instead he deflected attention over and over by saying he was not the Messiah. Throughout John 1, John uses different metaphors to point attention to Jesus. John says Jesus is the light, and he is the one who baptizes with the spirit, that he is the lamb of God. People looked to John at first for instruction. Like Princess Lea pointing to Poe in the Last Jedi, John the Baptist pointed to Jesus and said, "Don't look at me, follow him."

While John looked like a rebel, Jesus looked like he was nothing special, he kind of looked like everyone else. He dressed normally, socialized with sinners, he walked and looked humble. Yet he spoke like a radical. He spoke with unusual ideas, with authority, preformed miracles and rebelled against all sorts of orders of the day.

John tells us that the true light that gives light was coming into the world. Future tense. The Messiah hadn't arrived yet. The next sentence of our scripture tells us Jesus was in the world but that the world didn't know or recognize him. He came to his own but his own didn't accept or receive him. Just because Jesus came into the world, unless people are open to receiving and recognizing him, they were still waiting for the messiah to come. So, the people had to wait.

John 16 tells us we are scattered, to our own homes. And have to wait. We know that during this period all too well.

We may not always like it, but humans are accustomed to waiting.

Human life begins with waiting for nine months. Ask any expectant mother, and waiting for a delivery is not easy.

Advent is about our waiting for the Christ child to be born at Christmas. Much as Isaiah and other prophets wrote about Israel's waiting for a messiah. Children begin to grow, and they see presents around the tree and they want to open them, but must wait.

We grow up and wait in lines, in traffic and online for our internet to unfreeze.

We have activities we'd like to do and actions we'd like to take but we have to wait.

Each of us are waiting for something in our lives or job or school or relationship.

Each of us are waiting for something. We wait for an employer to email us back.

Waiting for a medical test.

Waiting for a health relationship.

Waiting is a spiritual disciple.   We wait for redemption.

So, we wait.

Especially this year.

I saw a T-shirt recently that read "The best quote ever is 'Life is short. Eat dessert first.'" Life is short. Eat dessert first. Put the last stuff, the best stuff, the enjoyable stuff, first when we can. That is not bad advice. Especially in a year that has been short on many extras for us and so much waiting.

That is what our family did one afternoon. We walked in the cold to downtown Bethesda at 5:00 to Jenni's Ice Cream, where I ate a delightful waffle cone of white chocolate peppermint. It was wonderful but kind messed up my dinner. But every once in a while, I like to eat dessert first.

There is actually interesting theology in this quote. Jesus puts dessert first in the Sermon on the Mount. It begins with the benediction. Usually we have benediction at the end of things, but Jesus begins that sermon with the beatitudes which are like a benediction. "Blessed are those who…." In the Book of Ephesians, Paul puts the benediction, the blessing, up front in verse 3.

Putting dessert first is what the season of Advent does. Advent begins with the end. Advent is the beginning of the liturgical year. On the first Sunday of Advent the lectionary gives us the ending. It suggests scriptures about Jesus returning on clouds descending. We don't always focus on the 2nd coming of Jesus, but it's an important part of Advent. Advent starts with the ending of the story, with Jesus' returning. Advent means arrival, the arrival of Jesus again to make all things new. The great victory of God in the end. Our hope is assured because Jesus returns, the dessert comes first, and so all the rest of the Christian story throughout the year, with John the Baptist pointing the way to the Messiah whose birth we celebrate in the Christmas manger, is heard with the backdrop that we know how the story ends. God wins. We start Advent with the dessert coming first.

In a year when so much has been put on hold, when we have been scattered, in our own homes, when we have been waiting, waiting for dessert to be served at all, Advent gives us permission to remember that no matter how dark and difficult and challenging things can seem, we can have hope.

The true light, that gives light to everyone, is coming into the world.

We testify and witness to that light by receiving the gift that Christ's light shines in our own lives. So, the gift of waiting, waiting for Christmas, waiting for the Messiah to return, waiting for the vaccine, waiting for things to return to normal, waiting for salvation, is that we might as well, we might at least, eat the Advent dessert now. That is to seize the hope and faith that God wins in the end, so you are freed to notice how the light of Christ is shining in your life now, even in the darkness of this time.

For Jesus has conquered the world. The Holy Spirit will come and be with us.

One of the most comforting things during this Covid experience to me has been the myriad of ways that many of you have shared of what your waiting during the pandemic has allowed you to discover how the light is shining in your life. What the light has illuminated in your own journey.

One person wrote to me how during this pandemic they developed a love of art and painting. They wrote that "I walk seeing beautiful visions and the hope of recreating them in some form, and it crowds out the doom and gloom and fears. I can only attribute this transformation to the grace of God."

I have loved several pandemic pictures which several folks have sent to me as the ways light has shined on parts of their life.

Some have written about how during this time they have read books that they otherwise wouldn't have read. Some on fault lines of American culture, some on racial justice. Others are reading Huckleberry Finn or Charles Dickens for the first time.

For me, I have been grateful for the time with family, playing chess, decorating the tree, and with it the appreciation that even when things are dark like this time, there is humor at home.

One shared that they have turned to the Psalms during this time. That the Psalms speak to us more now than at any time since 9/11. One turned to Psalm 27 in particular.

Psalm 27 beings with "The LORD is my light and my salvation — whom shall, I fear? Christ is our light and our salvation.

The Psalmist prays, "Teach me your way, LORD, lead me in a straight path." We know John the Baptist called on people to " make straight the paths of the Lord," quoting from Isaiah but also, in part, from Psalm 27.

Then the Psalmist ends with, "I will see the goodness of the LORD in the land of the living. Wait for the LORD, be strong and take heart, and wait for the LORD."

You and I are called to be take heart this year. We must be resolute. Take heart, the light is coming. Wait for the Lord. Engage in acts of giving and hope. Look to the light shining on your life. Be patient for the coming of salvation. Have the hope of knowing the end brings restoration, and holiness.

Friends, when we invest in our faith not knowing when our faith will be rewarded, we experience the sacred waiting of discipleship.

When we wait for the Lord, have hope, are confident that we will see the goodness of the Lord in the land of the living, we experience of sacred waiting of discipleship.

When we look not our own actions or the rebellious words of others but stay focused on the light of Christ shining in new ways in our lives, we experience the sacred waiting of discipleship.

When we look to the future, when we care about our church and our ministries in gratitude to all those who have made them possible over the years, and yet look to the future generations as we patiently plant seeds and patiently watch them grow, we participate in the sacred waiting of discipleship.

We can be impatient people. We want things to come quickly for us. Yet learning to wait for holiness, restoration, and salvation is a sacred gift of discipleship. It is the gift for God's people. It may be the holiness, the gift, that helps us make it through this scattered time.

As we recognize, receive, and make room for the true light that gives light to everyone and that is coming into the world.

So take courage; Jesus has conquered the world!

Let us pray. *Loving God, help us be open to your preparing the way for holiness, for our hope. May we wait for it in hope. Amen.*

John 17

In John 17 Jesus prays for his disciples. He was always caring for and about others. Jesus sought to walk in our shoes, to pray to God and to show moral leadership.

I have been reflecting on models for moral leadership at a time when national leadership is needed. I have been thinking about John Lewis. John Lewis was a pastor, civil rights leader, and representative from Georgia for many years.

He died not long ago, and with our focus as a nation on the need for racial justice, his legacy and work has gotten increased attention.

In his bestselling biography of John Lewis, His Truth Is Marching On, John Meacham writes that he considered Lewis a saint in the classic Christian sense. A good person, was in the church, did great things and even acted with martyrdom, sustaining significant injuries while standing up for justice on the Edmund Pettus Bridge in Selma, Alabama in the 1960's.

Some of the most powerful parts of Meacham's and other's observations of Lewis, talk about the inspiration of his Christian faith. Meechan talks about how Lewis approached the world and taught us to "open our arms, not to clench our fists."

Lewis was one of those rare leaders who was respected and loved by people on both sides of the aisle.

That reality came from his ability to put himself in another's shoes. To see their perspectives and appreciate ideas beyond his own.

The 2007 documentary of Lewis entitled Come Walk in My Shoes, follows his emotional pilgrimage to the churches, places, and bridges where he and others played an important role in the struggle for justice and equality.

The name for the documentary comes from Lewis' own words. When I google "best known John Lewis quotes" #1 on that list which comes up is, "When people tell me nothing has changed, I say come walk in my shoes."

That is helpful to note that when we despair about our present circumstances, to know that things can change. Lewis meant that in his lifetime, he had seen things improve. If people walked in his shoes, he could show them change. If they walked with him, alongside him, they would see something special. If we are to do something about racial justice, we do well to walk in another's shoes.

Jesus came to John to be baptized. John said that Jesus should baptize him. Yet Jesus insisted and was baptized by John in the water. Jesus invited John to walk in his shoes. To be the one baptizing. Jesus allowed John to do to him what Jesus would be doing, baptize. Jesus accepted John's baptism, which was called baptism for the forgiveness of sins, even though Jesus himself had no need to be forgiven of sins. Jesus invited John to walk in his shoes.

This is in part because in baptism, Jesus comes to walk in our shoes. The reason Jesus was baptized was to identify with us. In baptism, Jesus shared in our experience of baptism and life, much as he would later share in the human experience of death.

God would go to great lengths to walk in our shoes, we should do so with one another.

It tells us something about God. A God who chooses to come to us as a baby, in the circumstances of the manger, of Mary and Joseph and of the shepherds, has to be a God of mercy and compassion and vulnerability. That is one way we know we follow a God of love. So, it makes sense that this God would come to be with us in Jesus, to identify with us in baptism and to invite us to walk in His shoes.

To put self in another's shoes takes humility. It takes courage. It takes confidence. This is what our society needs now. We need people who are able to see selves in someone else.

One good friend who recently said, "One often hears it said that we are living in a new moment in the history of politics, in which for the first time it is becoming possible to imagine the existence of durable democratic regimes that are genuinely multicultural. That means regimes populated with people who vary widely in their most fundamental beliefs but still are able to live and work together because of none of the beliefs in question are given a privileged role in public life." For democracy to survive we need people who can put themselves in someone else's shoes. We need to be humble about our own judgements. We need to be willing to see the world a bit from another person's perspective.

We must keep in mind all humans are beloved and created in the image of God. Take seriously one's own religions views, but also the deepest convictions about people made in image of God. That is needed this week.

We are one nation. Can we say we that we draw some lines? Some things are not ok. Some things are not. We have to have some standards.

Matthew tells us that when Jesus invited John to walk in his shoes and baptize him, then they saw the spirit of God coming from Heaven and landed on him. It came close. So close that they could tell it was a dove.

This is the key for democracy. It's important to learn to be close. Now we think about people sorting into differently communities. Who are separated. Who are siloed. Today too many of us watch our own news or social media. People of differing backgrounds only living near people of similar outlooks. We realize that polarization is a problem. Many only read their own Facebook or Twitter or social media feed.

We need to be close. John Lewis' invitation to walk in his shoes was an invitation to get close. To see and not look away from people of differing perspectives.

The invitation of Jesus was an invitation to get close. The spirit descends on us too at our baptism. What does baptism mean in this context? It means we humans are touched by God. It means the human experience is impacted by the divine. The baptism message is not that we are untouchable. We are mortal. Covid proves that. But we are also touched by God and never alone. That God draws close. That we are all make in the image of God. That we are forgiven. It means we are called, called to love as ministers as Jesus claims us in baptism.

We cannot walk the exact path of Jesus. Yet he can carry us. As God draws near to us in baptism, we are called to follow him. Jesus said, "Pick up your cross and follow me. John wrote, "Whoever claims to live in him must walk as Jesus did." Peter said, "Christ also suffered for us, leaving us an example, that you should follow his steps."

It is not easy. Only Jesus can take away our sin. Baptism was Jesus' first step towards crucifixion. By taking on our sin, he opens the way for us to have a new way of living. For us to be unified with our Lord.

It is not easy, but we should try to walk in his shoes. And we do that by trying to get close. But studying him, praying to him, and following him as best we can.

God would go to great lengths to walk on in our shoes, so we should do so with one another.

As one African proverb talks of a man walking and seeing someone walk toward them, "When I saw him from afar, I thought he was a monster. ... When were got closer, I thought he was an animal....When he got closer still, I recognized that he was a human. When we were face to face, I realized that he was my brother. ... " As John Lewis might have put it, "To see and not look away." As long as we keep people at a distance, we can categorize them as monsters or animals. When we draw close, we see someone is a human. Made in the image of God. A fellow child of God.

We would like to get close together, face to face. We long to. As we reopen in a post pandemic world, we can do so more and more.

When we get close, the spirit pulls us together. When we are face to face, we can see and not look away. Yet we are in a time when being face to face is what we long far but cannot do. We not allowed to in the age of Covid. We must stay away. But that is coming. We will be face to face. So, we remember as we prepare.

So, let us use this time to learn about and understand someone different from us. Let us find a way to create a country where everyone feels included. Let us remember who we are in Christ and try to walk in another's shoes.

We have to remember our baptism. That in Christ, God came to be in our violent world, to walk in our shoes, so that we could walk in his. So, we could remember we are all made in God's image and called to respect others, understand them, and honor God's sacrifice for us.

We have to remember. Remember what happened January 6, 2021 so it doesn't repeat. Remember that democracy is fragile. That leadership matters. That we all have a role to play.

We have to remember that we are called to be close. We can't forget that we are called to be connected. We cannot forget what it's like to be back in our churches or doing projects together. We have to remember our baptism. When we baptize a child, we are called to remember our baptism. All of us are made in the image of God.

We have to remember, remember our past, remember our friends, remember our God. We are all loved by God. Baptism affirms that. Remember your baptism. Perhaps our remembering our baptism can help us re-member our divided nation and world. It could be that an effort to try and walk in another's shoes, or at least understand another's perspective, is what saves our democracy.

At his baptism, Jesus is given a new name. Beloved.

At our baptism we are given a new name as well - Christian. It reminds us that we are beloved. By God. Each of us worthy of love. And called to show it to each other. Baptism occurs when infants to let us know we are loved by God before we can respond. We don't earn salvation or Gods love we receive it. We are called beloved Christian at our baptism. Christian. One who acts in Christ's name, walks in his shoes, and seeks to walk in their neighbor's shoes.

John said he wasn't worthy to carry Jesus' sandals. But he did agree to walk momentarily in his shoes. By baptizing Jesus, he took on the mantle of doing work in Jesus name.

Jesus is saying, "For this particular time. Walk in my shoes." That is what Jesus says to us too. We need to do that now. For our time. When we baptize, we act in Jesus name. When we take communion, we do so in remembrance of him as it says on the inscription on our communion table at my church. When we love, we do so in Jesus' name. When we care we do so in Jesus' name.

Jesus who came to walk in our shoes. Bravely as a moral leader. And when we needed it most, to pray for us.

We need people who would walk in other's shoes.

We need people who seek to understand others and walk in their shoes.

The world needs people willing to do things in Jesus' name. The world needs people willing to try and walk in his shoes. Our nation needs people willing to open their arms. The world needs people who are willing to get close. The world needs people who know they are beloved and willing to live out that calling. The world needs people willing to think about walking in other shoes and inviting others, like John Lewis. The world needs people who will walk in another's shoes.

Usually, at our annual Baptism of the Lord Sunday services, we have a moment after the sermon, called the response in faith. Where we ask people to come up to the baptismal font. We turn to each other in line and make the sign of the cross on each other's forehead and say, "Remember your baptism and let the river of God's love flow through you." We couldn't touch each other's heads during Covid.

So, this past year, we didn't sign someone's head. We tried to walk in their shoes. As disciples of one who walked in ours.

Let us pray. *Loving God, be with our broken world. Heal our nation. Help us to walk together and follow your lead, remember our baptism as children of Christ, called to follow him and walk in each other's shoes. Amen.*

John 18

Denying discipleship is something we all do at times. Fortunately, God grants us grace.

John 18 tells us that Peter denied Jesus three times. We read,

"Simon Peter and another disciple were following Jesus. Because this disciple was known to the high priest, he went with Jesus into the high priest's courtyard, but Peter had to wait outside at the door. The other disciple, who was known to the high priest, came back, spoke to the servant girl on duty there and brought Peter in." "You aren't one of this man's disciples too, are you?" she asked Peter. He replied, "I am not."

And then Peter denied Jesus two more times. They had asked him, "You aren't one of his disciples too, are you?" He denied it, saying, "I am not."

We all deny God at times.

We all deny Jesus as Peter did. Fortunately, Jesus forgives us. Gives us a second chance. And calls us to make the most of it by telling our story. So that we might fulfill our calling as Christ's disciples.

This past year, Christ has been with us at home. Christ is with us here. Christ is always up ahead of us. Changing our focus. Raising us to share in repentance, reliance, reconciliation. Calling us to compassion and service. Calling us to follow. To feeling. To freedom.

To speak, because we have first been spoken to. We call because we have been called. We tell our story because God has included us in the great story of Jesus Christ.

The great story of Pentecost from Acts 2 begins with people from diverse areas gathering and the Holy Spirit enters their lives and gives them the ability to speak differing languages. It was so unusual that people around them thought they had been drinking. So, Peter stood up and explained what really was happening. That the Holy Spirit came to the people just as the prophet Joel had once predicted.

Peter shared God's plan, described the good news of Jesus Christ's death and resurrection, talked about what King David had said, and gave the people instructions about what they should do. It was incredible sermon and three thousand people joined the church that day.

Peter gave a message with great passion and authenticity. His speaking was effective because of what Peter said in Acts 2 verse 32. That he and others were witnesses to Jesus. They talked about what they knew and had seen and had experienced through the spirit. They testified to what they had participated in. We cannot give away what we haven't received. Peter was able to tell that story because he was given a story to tell. He was called to speak because Jesus had spoken to him.

The author of Acts is Luke, the same person who is the writer of the Gospel of Luke. In Luke 5 we read that Jesus gives Peter a charge, a story to tell, a calling. Peter is unsuccessfully fishing with others when Jesus appears, helps them catch many fish and then gives Peter a spiritual calling.

Jesus calls Peter to fish for people. Peter demurs at first, arguing that he wasn't worthy, but Jesus calls him anyway. Peter's life was changed by a calling from Jesus. He now had a new story. A new calling.

His story was to fish for people. At Pentecost, Peter got his chance. He spoke up, about the good news of Jesus Christ and 3000 people joined the church. He had become a fisher of people. He was fulfilling his calling. He spoke of what he had witnessed. He spoke about his story. He talked about what he himself had faith in.

One of the most challenging things we do as Christians is speak about our faith. So, like Jeremiah and Moses, Jonah, Isaiah, and many others we resist God's call to speak up. We think we are too young too old not well read enough or too busy or too risk adverse to share our story. Like Peter we sometimes lack confidence to do so. Like Peter we feel things haven't gone well in the past. We have failed. We have sinned. Or we feel we aren't worthy of speaking up. It's too much attention. We will mess it up or offend.

It can be risk to speak up. Peter takes a risk of dropping everything to follow Jesus. It isn't until later, at Pentecost, when Jesus has already ascended, when Peter sees the fruit of his labors. Yet we don't do it to be rewarded. We do it because like Peter, we are called. We are called by a God who didn't do hard things on a cross for us to stay on the sidelines, but to get into the arena. If we don't take a risk to speak up, things won't get better.

As we come back together from Covid, this is a time of great opportunity for the community of faith. That is what the early church folks wanted. They wanted to find meaning especially once Jesus had ascended. Peter talked to them about what he knew. He had been to the empty tomb. John tells us that Peter had seen risen Christ. Luke says he spoke confidently because he had personal experience. His story made his sharing the good news of Jesus credible authentic and powerful.

There is personal growth that can happen in our time by our speaking of faith. Telling our story. With authenticity and vulnerability. Not staying too much general or surface or shallow. But sharing what is our deepest desire of the heart. Where have we encountered God in it. Peter who had denied Jesus, was given a second chance. So, he came with a powerful testimony of faith. Not a story of division or stereotypes of people who are different but an inclusive, loving, attractive place to find hope and call home.

There is a very strong connection between our scripture in Luke 5 and Jesus' encounter with Peter in John 21. Many details during these the miraculous catch of fish stories are the same. But John 21 is a post resurrection appearance of Jesus while Luke 5 depicts the similar story as part of Peter's call to discipleship.

After his resurrection, Jesus tells Mary to go to Peter and share the good news. How excited must Peter has been? He was given a second chance. The good news was for him. And then he was given a calling.

The theological implication is that there is a connection between our call to discipleship and our call to speak and act in Jesus name now about his good news. We are forgiven. We are called to be his disciple and follow him. But also, to speak and act in his name by doing his mission out in the world. Service in connecting with real people in the world.

We are called to share our story because God has spoken to us in the life of Jesus Christ. For its God's story ultimately. Bigger than any other. We are part of it. When we tell our own stories, God is with us in them. As God has been present with so many others over the years. We have been given this opportunity, to tell God's story here.

We all have a story to tell. Like Peter, we have moments where God has spoken to us. Tell those stories. With each other and with the world. As Peter found, the deep stories, the personal tales, of how we came to follow Jesus, are powerful. They are unique. They are you. Tell your story. The world needs them.

We sometimes feel like we should speak about faith, and we are fishing for what to say. Someone asks us about our church or something personally and we feel like we are casting a line. Someone asks us about God, and we feel we are in deep water, over our heads. Just speak about your experience. Testify to what you know. Talk about what you have witnessed. The passion that comes from personal testimony is what makes imperfect people like Peter and us successful.

As we come back together, tell your stories of what happened during Covid. Stories of holy moments, sacred studies, divine encounters, and holy gatherings, with each other. Where you found and find God, reconciliation, and transformation. Share your story with the world. The world wants to know if the church still matters. That God is still involved in our time. That there is holiness in the world. For every time someone tells their unique story of faith it is another drop of grace, a testament that God isn't distant, but active and involved in our world.

You have a unique story to tell. One of power and history and faith. As you come back together, how has this year impacted you? Tell that story.

We all deny Jesus as Peter did as times. Fortunately, Jesus forgives us. Gives us a second chance. And calls us to make the most of it by telling our story. So that we might fulfill our calling as Christ's disciples.

You have a unique calling, unique experience, unique gifts, no one has your exact testimony.

No one can replace your unique voice. I love how our DCE Matt once put it to the youth, "there is a place in the church, which only you can fill."

You have a unique story to tell. Tell it.

Let us pray. *Loving God, help us to share our faith, our passion, our story, with you, each other, and the world. Let us do so in faith. In the name of the savior we pray. Amen.*

John 19

We disciples are empowered. For the source of our strength is not this world. It comes from above. And also, it is within us.

As I mentioned at the beginning of this work and say again, my sense of the heart of our faith is that Jesus is our savior, who offers us eternal life and a right relationship with God. Our teacher, who offers us abundant life and a right relationship with ourselves. Our connector, who calls us together into the church and offers us a right relationship with each other and the world, empowered by the holy spirit. We think, moreover, in part about having right relationships with ourselves.

John 19 shares that Jesus tells Pontius Pilate at his trial saying, "You would have no power over me if it were not given to you from above." Jesus made clear his power didn't come from this world. That he had transcended this world. He represented peace and holiness and truth they could not take away. Pilate had no power over Jesus either.

The guards did "take Jesus away" to his crucifixion. Yet they didn't take him away fully. For there is a kingdom of God within us that no one can take away.

How would Jesus continue to be with his disciples, even if he was taken away? Because through the Holy Spirit, part of the kingdom of God is within us.

If his kingdom is not of this world, then where is it? It comes from above. Yet it is within us.

We often think about the kingdom of heaven. The Book of the Revelation speaks to the kingdom to come at the end of times. Each Advent we celebrate Jesus coming on clouds descending to remake the world. In the Lord's Prayer we confess of "Thy Kingdom come."

Jesus speaks of power from above and of a kingdom of God which is within us. While we have trouble seeing that kingdom, we can feel it. The idea of a kingdom of God being within us implies an inside, internal connection to God. The idea of God within us implies that there is a holy part of us. A part which stays with us, is portable, that no one can take it away, which can be our connection to God. They cannot take this part of Jesus away from his followers.

There is a kingdom of God within us that no one can take away. Our challenge and opportunity is to embrace the truth that there is a kingdom of God within us.

Despite our human imperfections, problems, and sinfulness, we have the spark of God within us.

I believe in the idea of a soul. Of a holy part of ourselves, gifted by God. A deep holiness within us, which lasts, even as the body decays, and will be reunited when all things are made new.

The more we are able to focus on that soul, that holiness within us, the calmer and healthier we can be.

Now, just because Jesus says his kingdom is not of this world doesn't mean this world around us doesn't matter. Christians affirm that Jesus is our king now. He will come again to remake the world. That, as Paul suggests, the body, the physical world, matters. We pray "thy will be done now on earth as it is in Heaven," caring about this world.

Russian dissident Leo Tolstoy famously wrote a 19th century book entitled "The Kingdom of God is Within You." Banned in Russia and printed in Germany, this book included principles of nonviolence which Tolstoy believed Jesus required. That in this kingdom Jesus' followers would not need to fight for him. Mahatma Gandhi called it one of the two most influential books on his thinking. It heavily influenced members of the American civil rights movement of the 1960's. Tolstoy writes that the kingdom of God is one of love. It is the love of God which places the divine holiness within us. In John's Gospel, we get a vision of Jesus' kingdom which is based, not on ideals of this world, but on self-giving love. Tolstoy believed that Jesus' ideas about the internal kingdom which impacted our world here.

For example, part of our opportunity then is to think of a right relationship with ourselves before we venture out to do God's work in the world.

Well, Pilate responds to Jesus' statement here asking, "You say you are a king then?" Jesus says, "You say I am a king."

What makes Jesus a king is that he rules in our hearts. As a wonderful anthem puts it, "the soul is Christ's abode." His throne includes our pure hearts.

Most of us need some help now. With anxiety, depression, fear, isolation rising to alarming levels. That half of Americans report the pandemic is harming their mental health and a federal emergency hotline for people in emotional distress registered a 1000% increase in calls this past spring.

We, like the men in Luke's Gospel, are facing serious issues. We need somewhere we can go when all else around us seems so hard. Yet during this time, where can we go? It has been hard to get on airplanes. We can't go on vacations as we like. Many of us can't go to school or our offices. We can't even go to church.

Yet our faith can help make us well, for the internal part of us, the heart, the soul, the holy center of God, can be part of the healing.

How do we have right relationships with ourselves? Paul wrote to the Colossians, "Let the peace of Christ rule in your hearts."

Discipleship is the act of following Jesus. Of following him by making him the king of our lives. If you are considering being Jesus' disciple, the part of his reign I suggest you consider, is letting the peace of Christ rule in our hearts. Now how do we get to that?

This is where pushing out distractions matter. Thomas Merton and other great mystics defined solitude is an uninhabited place. A place we can go physically or spiritually which is uninhabited by distractions.

We find the kingdom of God within us when we push away the distractions around us, and then connect with the holy inside us.

One of my mentors likes to say, "It's a practice, an art, a discipline, to learn to let go of all that takes us away from the God within."

And the more we are able to remove the distractions from our lives, the more in touch with that core, that center, that holiness within us we can be.

This has been a personal challenge for me. It's not just as easy as shutting a door in a room. I have been trying to pray at night to push out the distractions I face in order to focus on the holy within me. I have been trying to do it. To let the king reign of rule in my hearts. And it's a challenge. But practice, discipline helps. And God wants to provide us that help.

When we seek to push out distractions, we are able to listen to the voices we need to hear. We can hear what God is saying to us when we embrace the solitude. This is perhaps a gift of this Covid time, to be able to embrace the solitude and the lack of being inhabited spaces in our world, and to listen to the voice of God within us.

One book I've found helpful during this Covid time is "Practice in the Presence of God" by a 17th century French monk named Brother Lawrence. Lawrence writes, "We'd be surprised if we knew what our souls say to God sometimes." An internal, holy dialogue. Lawrence implies a deeper sense of the presence of God in us. That the part of us that God has gifted us longs to connect with God, to communicate with God, to pray with God. A place when all distraction is gone.

That is a tough goal. Books can point us, but we have to actually do it.

This is where spiritual practices matter to help us let go of all the things that keep us from full attentiveness to the God within us. Meditation. Prayer. Lectio Divina. Centering prayer. Letting go of what is on outside and paying attention to the presence of God within us moves us towards communion. All the practices that are about letting go of all that separate you from God.

Letting go of our conditioned responses. Being fully present to the spirit and not pushing away those parts of the spirit within us we don't like. Asking, where do I notice God? What would God have me do? Asking what is getting in the way of your attentiveness of to what is going on between you and God? Pay attention to what helps you let go of what gets in the way of the oneself with the God within us.

Let this time be one of developing the discipleship discipline of listening to God. The point of discipleship is to learn the practices, it to practice paying attention to God.

Jesus gets our attention. God in a form we can relate to gets our attention.

The good news is the kingdom of God is always within you. There is a soul is within you. There is holiness is within you. Your power comes from above and is within you.

We become more in touch with the soul within us when we move away the distractions. In that we find God. We discover the peace of Christ ruling our hearts. We find healing.

Luke records Jesus saying that kingdom of God is within you. Many translations of the Bible render the Greek that Jesus is saying the kingdom of God is "among you." That the context here is of Jesus talking to the Pharisees and referring to himself, telling the Pharisees in Luke's Gospel that his coming into the world brings the kingdom. But what about the context of Jesus' arrest, when he was about to be gone?

This is where the value of the soulful, the holiness of God, matters perhaps most, for the kingdom of God within helps connect us to the truth.

When Jesus ends this section of John's Gospel, he says "for this I came into the world, to testify to the truth. Everyone who belongs to the truth listens to my voice."

Truth is an important theme in John's Gospel. It appears 25 times. Much more than the other Gospels. It remains to guide Jesus' disciples, even when Jesus was gone. God is our compass, Jesus is our north star, the one whom wise men followed a star to find, and the holy spirit is our guide. Truth is a matter of doing what is right.

We know the truth of something in our hearts. And when Jesus is there in our heart, we find truth.

John tells us Jesus says a few chapters earlier, "I am the way and the truth and the life." For John, the truth of Jesus is not a series of principles to be articulated, but a person to be followed. Jesus is the truth. How we act in following him shows, for John, if we understand that truth. Jesus is the truth. And a few chapters before that John tells us that the truth shall set us free. Jesus is the truth, the fulfillment of ancient prophecy, the culmination of what is right, the unity of things just feeling right in our hearts. So, discipleship, the following of Jesus, matters in experiencing and living out the truth. For there is a kingdom of God within us that no one can take away.

As I have mentioned before, I have been inspired by the story of Bryan Stevenson (see his excellent book, *Just Mercy*, or Warner Bros. 2019 film by the same name or the Equal Justice Initiative), a Harvard educated lawyer who heads to Alabama to defend those wrongly condemned or those not afforded proper representation. One of his first cases is that of Walter McMillian, who is sentenced to die in 1987 for the murder of an 18-year-old girl, despite evidence proving his innocence. In the years that followed, Stevenson encounters racism and legal and political maneuverings as he fights for McMillian's life.

At one low point in the journey, Stevenson appears to have lost the legal appeal for McMillian and has indirectly gotten his son in trouble. Stevenson laments to McMillian he believed he had just made things worse.

But McMillian reassured him, saying that Stevenson "helped him get his truth back." That even if he loses his life, he "will go down smiling." That being in jail for many years and hearing the other side say he was guilty; he began to doubt himself. That maybe those who had lied and wrongly convinced him were correct. He started to think maybe he was guilty. But in the process of Stevenson showing a court the evidence that McMillian was innocent, he gave McMillian his truth back.

They both needed to be right with themselves before they could do the justice work to which they were called. They needed to refocus on the truth.

He reminded him of what is right and wrong. That he was right and innocent. McMillan told Stevenson, "You gave me my truth back. You gave it to me, to me and my family. And no one can take that away from me."

Our world needs truth more than ever today. Our national dialogue needs the truth more than ever. Our politics needs truth. Pilate asked Jesus, "What is truth?" Too many folks online or in power or in person are trying to obscure the truth in our day too.

Yet Jesus affirms that he is the way the truth and the life. That he came to testify to the truth through his life. For the peace of Christ in our hearts is not only what is holy, but it what is true.

If the kingdom of God is within us, it makes our daily lives more holy. Today is holy. This moment is holy. You are holy. The soulful sense, natural law, gut feeling, our inherent sense of right and wrong is in our hearts. Perhaps we need to rediscover it. It can begin by looking deep within ourselves.

It's hard to see the holiness of this time. But amidst the brokenness, the idea of the kingdom of God being within us, allows us to reclaim holiness within the brokenness.

As we seek to be disciples, know that it begins with our recognizing the kingship of Jesus. Yet his kingdom is not of this world. It will come someday to remake the world.

To be able to make a difference, we need to be right with ourselves. When we have trouble doing that, we can draw on the knowledge that there is a kingdom of God is within us. There is holiness within you. Push away the distractions and embrace that. Get in touch with the God inside you.

We disciples are empowered. For the source of our strength is not this world. It comes from above. And so, it is within us. The things of the world cannot constrain us.

Christian Followership

There is holiness, truth, a kingdom of God within you, and no one can take that away.

Let us pray. *Loving God, allow us to tap into your power which comes from above. Help us to seek, find and honor your kingdom within us. Amen.*

John 20

John 20 contains the story of the resurrection and it is a most special chapter. Especially for Jesus' disciples.

Easter is a celebration of God's love. A triumph of love over death. John writes that God is love. That love is from God. That Christ, who is close to the Father's heart, makes God known.

Easter is our discovery that love doesn't end with death. The ancient assumption was that the experience of love we feel in life would end with death. Easter shows otherwise. We often read from John 20 on Easter.

Jesus lived a life of love. Welcoming children. Healing the sick. Yet he was unjustly put to death. For those who followed him, during his three days in a tomb, evil seemed to have won. Then on Easter, the tomb was empty. Jesus rose from the grave, appeared and continued to love those around him. Death could not stop God's love.

When I worry about my hope for eternity, let me tell you what resurrects my belief that love is stronger than death. John's Gospel tells us there were three people present around the resurrection. Mary Magdalene, Peter, and an unnamed disciple. Their experience shows that God's love can lead to belief, overcome sin, and change our lives.

Nowhere in Scripture is the resurrection itself directly described. What we do have is the testimony of people around it and to whom Jesus appeared afterwards. The resurrection happened without video footage. God did it, but we have to internalize it. We must decide to believe it.

History suggests to me and others that the resurrection happened. As a recent CNN special indicates, there is a historical consensus that Jesus lived and died. People at the time saw the risen Lord and staked their lives on it. If the resurrection were made up, they would not have chosen these witnesses. Homicide detective Warner Wallace, who had investigated many crimes in California and won awards for his work, began investigating the gospels as eyewitness accounts to Jesus. Wallace was an atheist and skeptic, but the more he studied the resurrection the more he concluded it was true. Wallace used the same rigorous methods on Jesus' resurrection that he did on homicide cases. He concluded that based on the historical record, the resurrection of Jesus is a fact of history. He became a follower of Christ and regular church attender as a result.

At Easter, God gives us a glimpse of God's attitude and the character of God's transformative love in the world.

The presence of love in our world, in all its forms, despite our ills, love which scripture tells us is from God, helps me believe there is something after death.

People from Dorothy Day to Billy Graham have described the birth of babies as proof not only that God exists, but that a loving God exists. On Good Friday, we had a two-week-old join us for our afternoon service. What a reminder of new life in the midst of death.

Many have looked at the makeup of the universe to say science shows there must be a higher being. They ask, "Why would God create us for such a relatively short time on earth, unless that God had plans for us to be with God someday?" I don't believe God would go to the trouble of creating us or allowing us to continue without being a loving God. Everything we know about Jesus, who talked frequently about the coming kingdom of God, tells us God wants us to continue our relationship with God's love.

Who was the first disciple to believe the resurrection? It was the unnamed disciple, who is identified only as the "disciple whom Jesus loved." Love is a key to belief.

Read the scriptures on your own. Explore the heart of God for yourself. Open your soul to God's spirit. Think of the presence of love in our world. In our focusing on God's love, we find belief and faith.

We might say, ok, maybe the resurrection could have happened, but God couldn't possibly love someone like me. With all I've done? Resurrection couldn't be for me, could it?

A 1000 years ago, a theologian named Anselm wrote a famous essay, "Why God Became a Man," in which he argued that we humans disobey God and God's justice requires that sin be punished. Yet in God's grace, Jesus, God's own son, substitutes for our punishment. Jesus paid the price on the cross. He got what we deserved.

Ok, we might say, maybe the resurrection could have happened and maybe God is forgiving, but this can't possibly matter now. The resurrection happened so long ago. It can't impact my life. Love in our world may be more important now than ever.

Peter, you may recall, had denied Jesus three times when things got tough. Peter hung his head in shame. The resurrection gave him a second chance too. When Peter heard the news, he ran to the empty tomb. His believing that Jesus was alive changed his heart. It changed his life. Peter went from being a denier of Christ to being the leader who built the church.

God's love can impact how we think about our lives and the state of the world. Our focusing on the resurrection can change our life and in doing so change the world. Our believing in love more than death has never been more important.

St. Anselm's ideas shape classic Christian theology, the ideas of his contemporary named Peter, Peter Abelard, matter too. Abelard argued that Jesus' death and resurrection are less about substitutionary justice than about love.

Abelard was a French priest at Notre Dame. He had a love affair. She became pregnant. He was captured and tortured. They were relegated, he to a monastery, she to a convent, where they wrote each other letters for the rest of their lives.

Love changed Abelard's view of the resurrection. The resurrection changed his view of love. He concluded that the problem in Jesus death, and indeed our harsh world, was not too much sin, but too little love. Abelard wrote that Jesus came to show God's love and thus to awaken our love. He wrote, Jesus "bound us to himself in love, with the result that our hearts should be enkindled by a gift of grace." The power of Christ is to change the human heart.

Max Lucado defined grace as God as a heart surgeon, cracking open our chest, removing our heart - poisoned with pain - and replacing it with God's own. Such love is our hope for our world.

Easter reminds us that God's love for the world is not dead. It's connected to God's promise that death is not the end. I was sitting with a member of our congregation in the hospital last year. It was a challenging time. As we sat, we prayed Romans 8: 38-39, where Paul, who had faced death, concludes, "I am convinced that neither death nor life, nor anything else will be able to separate us from the love of God in Christ Jesus."

As I have had the privilege of being with people at the end of life, as they talk about people they loved and miss and look forward to seeing, my belief in the resurrection has increased. For even when the body fades, love remains. As we grieve for someone, our love for them continues. Nothing, not even death, separates us from God's love. That is why Paul concludes in 1 Corinthians 13, that love never ends.

This is the 30th anniversary of the film, *The Princess Bride* (20th Century Fox, 1987). Maybe you've seen it. I love that film. In it, Princess Buttercup thinks her love Wesley has died and so she becomes engaged to be married to someone she doesn't love. Wesley reappears and after Wesley and Buttercup roll down a bumpy hill, their identities are revealed, and Buttercup exclaims, "Wesley, you're alive!" Wesley says, "I told you I would always come for you. Why didn't you wait for me?" Then Buttercup very reasonably answers, "Well, you were dead." To which Wesley responds, "Death cannot stop true love. All it can do is delay it for a while."

Friends, we are saved by our own heavenly father's heart. The triumph of Easter is that death cannot stop love. Whether its three blocks or three days in a tomb, eventually love prevails.

Like the unnamed disciple, we can believe. Like Mary, we are forgiven. Like Peter, the resurrection can change our lives too.

For Jesus rose on Easter to shower us with grace. To save our eternal souls. To give us our lives new meaning. To transplant joy into our hearts. To bring hope to our world. To resurrect love for you and for me.

I received an email in mid-February 2021 telling me that as clergy, my group was up to get a Covid vaccine. So, I registered online. The next week I drove to the Six Flags mass vaccination site. I sat in my car for about two hours and when I got to the vaccine check in, I could tell that the person checking me in was having a tough day. He was using an iPad to check folks in using the bar code on my phone, and due to connectivity issues, he couldn't get it to work. He was not happy about it. He started cursing his iPad and yelling bad words and foul expletives over and over at it. He used just about every four-letter word in the book to express his feelings towards his faulty technology.

Finally, the man gave up on his iPad and decided to try and log me in a different way. So, he looked up and asked me pointedly, "What is your occupation?"

Now at this point I wasn't sure what to do. I wanted to make the poor guy feel better by answering something like, "My occupation? Oh, I'm a sailor… And part time football coach."

But I had to tell the truth, for the only reason I was in line at a mass vaccination site in February was because of my occupation. So, I looked sheepishly at the guy who had spent the last several minutes screaming profanities at his iPad and I said, "I'm a church pastor." The man stared at me, uttered one more expletive, and went to the next car.

There are some things that probably should be contained.

On the other hand, there are some things that are just too good to be bottled up. The good news is that because of Jesus Christ, God's love should not, need not, cannot and will not be contained.

The work of Christ on the cross is that of redemption and forgiveness for humanity. We see that through the experience of Peter, our representative and the rock upon whom Jesus built the church. Peter had denied Jesus three times. But God's messenger, the young man, tells the women to share the news with the disciples and Peter. Peter is mentioned by name because God wants it clear that the good news is for him, for us, for all, even those who doubt or fail or fret or fear. Peter and we, are forgiven, redeemed, loved.

Let Jesus become the cornerstone for you. Psalm 118 tells us that the stone that was rejected has become the chief cornerstone. Cornerstones were critical in ancient buildings because everything in the building rested on it. Peter, Petras, the rock, said that Jesus, whom the authorities of his time rejected, was the stone God used to be the cornerstone of salvation. Yours and mine.

Because the separation between God and us have been removed through Christ, we can have a different path, a new perspective, renewed strength to move around the stone, a second chance.

The good news of Easter, is that God has rolled away the stone. The tomb is empty, the body is gone, and Jesus is already out in the world, out where we are. Jesus brings a love that comes to us and goes to where we are, in our imperfection, to help us during our challenge, of our new opportunity.

This past year we have been afraid of the pandemic, for good reason. We have been overwhelmed by the reality of death from covid, and separation from loved ones. We have seen school learning deferred, job losses, the reality, as so many of us are awaking up to, of long time-suffering for many people simply because of the color of one's skin, and seniors confined to the bunker of facilities or homes.

Jesus goes out from the tomb into the reality of our pain to identity with us. With you. He enters into our fears to transform them. To bring us faith. He walks in our shoes, dies our death, and rises so we can rise again too. His steadfast love endures forever.

God loves us. In Jesus, God doesn't stay in the tomb. Jesus goes to great lengths to be with those he loves.

No matter what barriers or boundaries or obstacles or stones stand in our way, some love cannot be contained. Jesus leaves the tomb and goes to great lengths to be with those he loves.

That is like the love of the savior. That is the love of a God who comes to us at Christmas as a baby. Who lived as a servant on earth in order to be with us. Who gifts a spirit to leave a connection with us. Who shows us in Jesus Christ what sacrificial love is all about. So that we could be lifted up. So that we have the value of relationship when we are vulnerable. So that we too can go out into our corner of the world to express love which cannot be contained. And when we can't recall our faith, Jesus reminds us on Easter Sunday that God's love is larger than any pandemic, bigger than our fears, greater even than death itself.

If we have questions about whether we are worthy of God's love, or wonder if God will save people like us, or doubt whether Easter makes any difference in our lives, Mark's ending makes clear that Jesus is out in the world, our world. Out even in the deepest, darkest places of our souls. Even in the most remote corners of our hearts. Even with those of us who feel we have no need for Jesus, that we can be just fine if we work hard enough. He comes even to us, for eventually some things won't work and life will become difficult for us, and frustrating, and like Job we will consider yelling and cursing and carrying on. For them, for us and for always, there is Easter hope.

I reframed an anonymous poem to express how I, and maybe you too, might feel as we contemplate the promise of Easter during this time of Covid:

I used to stay inside my room, and felt perhaps I failed.
My same routine of fears and doubts, it seemed like I was jailed.
I longed so much to do the things that I had done before,
But I was stuck inside my tomb, a boulder at the door.

Then I heard the Easter promise that the stone was rolled away.

And Jesus goes before me now, inviting me today.

To walk with him and find that I am full and fair and free.

To claim the promise of my Lord, whose love is there for me.

Friends, accept the savior's offer to come to you, be with you, minister to you.

Believe that he can roll away the stones, the overwhelming obstacles from your life, so you too can be free.

Allow his gracious sacrifice to inoculate you against the overwhelming impact of failure or doubts or fears, including the fear of death.

Receive the holy spirit, so it can guide you out of your tomb, your bunker, into a world which needs your heart.

Let God's love, which cannot be contained, be your gift, this day and forever more.

Let us pray. *Loving God, help us believe. Help us to be honest with you. Speak your truth to us. So that we might believe. That we might proclaim. That we might live out the glory of your love. That your limitless love might be made real in the hearts of each of us. Amen.*

John 21

The work of discipleship continues. It is never-ending. The calling of Jesus' disciples after his resurrection is the calling of his disciples today. We are called to make sure that his work continues in his name. Let us embrace the calling and do that work as his disciples.

We are called to live out our calling as disciples of Christ. In the spirit of the resurrection, empowered by the living Christ. Yet the story does not end with the resurrection. That is just the beginning.

My kids are really into Marvels movies. *Avengers*. *Endgame* etc. There is great action in most of them. At the end of most of the Marvel films, there are what are called "post credit scenes." Once the action ends, the regular film, the credits rolls, and so the audience is incentivized to remain in the theater because of these post credit scenes. Scenes that hint at the future action of the films to come. So, in Avengers Infinity War, for example, the post credit scenes show Samuel L Jacksons character, Nick Fury, seeing a beeper with the symbol for Captain Marvel appearing, foreshadowing the appearance of Captain Marvel in her new film.

In John's Gospel, after Jesus' resurrection in John 20 which we read often at Easter, we expect the action to end. We expect the highpoint of the story to be the resurrection, as it is, and then the story ends. The last two verses of John chapter twenty, appear to bring the story to a conclusion, stating that Jesus did many other signs that could not be recorded in this book, calling on Christians to believe that Jesus is the Son of God and receive the life he offers.

But John's Gospel continues the action after the resurrection, as the story continues. "After these things, Jesus showed himself again to the disciples…" and John 21 starts, seemingly after the conclusion.

It seems a little out of place at first. Many scholars believe that it was written by another hand than the John who composed the rest of the Gospel.

Yet there is important purpose to John 21 and this post credit scene.

I think one reason why post credit scenes in movies are satisfying is that they represent something closer to real life than do the ending of many movies. Most movies end with a tight ending, the hero wins, the girl and boy meet, the bad guy gets what's coming to him, justice prevails. Our family has been reading and watching Alice in Wonderland recently. Its's a story that gets tied up pretty neatly as bad queen is defeated, and we realize Alice has been having a dream being in Wonderland. And she returns to reality.

In the Marvel films the post credit scenes remind us that the story continues. That is the way real life is. Life rarely gets tied up as neatly as in the movies. Real life has loose ends, lingering issues and ramifications for the heroes and others of their actions. It is more complex. The story often continues. Post credit scenes foreshadow what comes next.

John 21 is the final chapter of John's Gospel. We read it, almost working backwards in the story. Since this is the last Gospel written, this is perhaps the final chapter of the Gospels.

The post resurrection appearances in the Bible of Jesus, such as in John 21, remind us that gospels are more like real life than the movies. Real life is more unpredictable. Certainly, this past year has been unpredictable. With its virus and social distancing and stratification and disruption.

Life was complex and unpredictable for the disciples in John 21. They were on the run. Following Jesus, but then he was killed and then resurrected. After all the ups and down of following Jesus, the betrayal and Jesus' death and the empty tomb, the excitement of the resurrection was over for the disciples, and they return to the rhythms of fishing of all things. I can relate to that. Many of us have sacred places in the summer we tend to visit. For me that is in upstate New York. I was unable to visit it this year. I like to go fishing there.

"I'm going fishing," Peter says. "We'll go with you," answer the disciples. They didn't catch any fish at first.

In John 21, Jesus' third post resurrection appearances occurs on the Sea of Tiberias, also known as the Sea of Galilee. Not in the holy city of Jerusalem, but in the ordinary world of Galilee. Our work of discipleship take place in our ordinary lives.

Jesus gives the disciples some good advice about how and where to fish and they catch a lot of fish.

And they have a cookout on the beach. Not one too different from the scene at the feeding of the 5000. In that story, Jesus multiplied bread and fish so all the people could be fed.

Here there is enough to go around too. For John tells us there are 153 fish. There has been a lot of debate from scholars about the meaning of 153 but one interpretation, which a scholar named Jerome in the 4th century promulgated and many scholars subscribe to, is that is the total number of species of fish in the lake known at the time. In other words, everyone is represented and included.

That it took place in Galilee helps remind us that the story of Christ's love continues into the real lives that we lead. The work of the church continues. That all are included.

Even when one person dies, or moves, or a pastor departs, the work of the church continues, because it is God's work. God continues to watch over us, love us and lead us in God's own way.

After Jesus appears, Peter has a conversation with Jesus after his resurrection. In it, Peter is an every-person, a symbol of humanity, an agent who stands for you and me. For all of us. Peter is the one whom Jesus said, "upon him I will build my church." Peter's name, petros, means rock. On this rock, this foundation, Jesus says, I will build my church. And so, he did. The work for the church continued through Peter that day and through us.

In their famous, modest, but powerful discussion, Jesus three times asks Peter, "Do you love me." And each time Peter responds, "You know that I do Lord." This simply encounter is dripping with irony because not too long before Peter had three times denied Jesus.

Actually, at first, Jesus asks, "Do you love me more than these?" There are at least three interpretations of what Jesus means here. Jesus could mean, do you love me more than all the other disciples love me? Are you my favorite? Or Jesus could mean, do you love more than you love all these other disciples? Am I your favorite? Or Jesus could be talking about the fish. Or at least the fishing. Meaning, do you love me more than you love the life and occupation of fishing. Are you willing to give it up to follow me? There is a cost to discipleship.

Here the risen Christ three times asks do you love me. It reminds the disciples of Jesus' commandment in John 13 to love one another as I have loved you.

The Greek is interesting here because the first two times Jesus uses the word Agape for divine unconditional love. And Peter responds each time with Philio, friendship love. Then the third time Jesus also uses Philio. To me that represents how in Christ, God comes to meet us where we are. Moreover, at first Jesus asks, "Do you love me more than these?" Yet the second two times Jesus asks he drops the "more than these" and just asks, "Do you love me?" Jesus seems to sense Peter's limits and tailors his questions. It represents how God comes to us with love but if we are unable to express it in return in a way, God finds a way to come closer to us. To meet us where we are.

Jesus gives Peter, and us, some mission, purpose for our lives and, as Peter represents the church too.

We hear that if we love Jesus, we are to feed his lambs. Tend this sheep. Feed his sheep. These are the three simple commands Jesus gives Peter.

Feed my lambs, tend my sheep, and feed my sheep. The Greek here implies that by feeding my lambs, Jesus comes to take care of each other, particularly the young or vulnerable. To reach out in compassion and service. To provide food and help where it is needed. To be supportive of those who are hungry in body mind and spirit way who are vulnerable.

The Greek implies that to tend his sheep means to act as a shepherd, following Jesus the good shepherd. To help guide and lead those who would be his people.

To feed the sheep is to feed, help and support the more mature among us, not just lambs.

Christian Followership

The call to discipleship for Peter is ironic because on the night of Christ's arrest Peter rejected his role as a disciple. They asked him if he was one of Chris's disciples and he said no. He denied Jesus.

Yet here Peter affirms his identity as a disciple of Christ. And in doing so, seals for our sakes the missional need for us to act as disciples by feeding and leading too.

It is a moment where he is called into a new identity in Christ. Whenever we have a baptism, we affirm a new identity in Christ. The questions of baptism ended with a person affirming that they would fulfill their calling as a disciple of Christ.

That is what Peter did. Affirmed his calling as a disciple of Christ. By feeding Christ's lambs. By tending his sheep. Feeding his sheep.

We, as part of the Church of Jesus Christ, come here in spirit, technology, and person to affirm our commitment to be disciples of Christ. We do so coming with our imperfections and fears and dreams all wrapped up into one. But we come following in the footsteps of Peter, who was so far from perfect that he made a public denial of Jesus, three times, before this famous affirmation of faith. In this uncertain time, when so much has been taken from us and so much seems imperfect, it is comforting to know that this early disciple, commissioned for service, wasn't perfect either.

In the circumstances we find ourselves in, much like the unusual circumstance of Peter's time, we hear Jesus calling us and telling us that we are needed, needed by the world. We need to feed the vulnerable lambs, the hopeless and hurting and hungry ones in the world. We are called to tend the sheep, each of us are ministers, as our bulletins said, to provide vision in the world, a world crying for leadership and hope. We are called to feed the sheep. Honoring and supporting long time members and connecting all to the body of Christ.

And we are called to do all of this in love. In fact, we are called to do all of it because of love. As John tells us, Jesus said we love because we were first loved by God. Because God loves us in Christ. And we are called to respond with love. Do we love Jesus? Do we love Jesus? Do we love Jesus? Yes, we do. We are to feed the lambs and tend the sheep and feed the sheep. We are to do all in love.

Love those who are in our families, who are in our church. Who are in our community. Those who are in our world.

As the church approaches our mission and ministry, as we plan for and live out our calling, we do so in love. To brainstorm in big ways, to dig deep to deal with division, to find ways to help those left behind, to ensure the church is stable, strong, and saturated with selfless service to a world that needs it. We offer stability for the lambs. For we sacrifice for the sheep. We provide healing for the sheep. We as the church provide leadership and hope for the community and world.

We do all this because we are part of the post credit scene of Christ's story too. Jesus' resurrection has life giving power that we are called to embrace, feed off and honor as we face a broken and hurting world with love.

We live in the real world, the complex world where events can be surprising, yet where the work of Christ continues in our own post credit way. For the church at its best doesn't care about who gets the credit, as long as the ministry of Jesus Christ continues.

This story of Covid this past year will give way to another story on the other side. And the church will continue, because we are called to feed and tend during this crisis and always.

As we tend to and water seeds that have been planted, we do so with boldness and hope, with grace and joy. And above all with love. Taking hold of this opportunity, moment and identify as disciples of Christ, we pick up the mantel of Peter as imperfect people in an imperfect time.

The calling of Jesus' disciples after his resurrection is the calling of his disciples today. We are called to make sure that his work continues in his name. Let us embrace the calling and do that work as his disciples.

We do all because the tale of Christ's church continues. During and after the pandemic. That the work of discipleship goes forward. That we are part of that important work. The resurrection of Christ is not the end. But the beginning. For the story continues. May we be hopeful, purposeful, and grateful as we play our part.

Let us pray. *Loving God, in the midst of this challenging time, may your spirit connect us and make us one. So that your holy work may continue through us. Amen.*

Conclusion

This has been a most unusual time in the life of the world, nation, and church. The Covid-19 pandemic has upended work, families, life, and the church. This work of the church seeks to help Christians think about discipleship during this most unusual time. This pandemic time when we look at spiritual disciples and seek stability and hope when so much seems out of sorts.

We have been socially distant and outside of our churches. People have not been able to go into their sacred spaces. But that is ok. That is changing. And so the work of discipleship changes, and continues.

What discipleship means to me is that we find holiness not in a place, but in a person. In the person of Jesus Christ. And so, if we are stuck outside our building, we can still go to Jesus. We are outside our sanctuary; we can find refuge in Christ. We are distant, but in discipleship we find Jesus is close.

We find the sacred in our world. Discipleship is about finding the holy in a person, not a place.

In our savior. In the good shepherd. We don't dwell permanently in our sanctuary. We don't spend the night in the church. We won't dwell in the holy place. The holy one dwells in us.

We don't know exactly how the Covid era will end or what the world will look like exactly on the other side. Variants and mutations and other issues may extend it. Yet even if and when we emerge from our Covid distancing and return to church, how do we see our calling and our faith changing? Perhaps we can learn something about discipleship during this time that can help us when we return to the post pandemic world. That through discipleship, holiness can be found in a person, not any place. It is my hope that we all may find such holy peace in Jesus Christ. May it be so. Amen.

Epilogue

Our calling is to realize that our meaning, our "why" for being, our sacred purpose can be found in following Jesus as his disciples.

Mark Twain supposedly once said, "The two most important days in your life are the day you are born and the day you find out why." I love that quote.

There is a deep meaning to it. Different faith traditions talk about this idea in varying, but somewhat similar, ways. They say the first important day in life is about biology - the day of our physical birth, or when our soul gets a body, when we come into existence. Then they affirm that at some point we find our deeper meaning, a purpose to life, our "why".

Some of us may find our why in a job. Others in a family. All of us I believe will have a life-long search for the why of life. We will have some questions and moments of doubt our whole lives. We will have periods of deep faith and trust.

Some of us may find our "why" in a cause. Yet the main "why" of our tradition is found not in leading anything. But simply in following.

Our tradition holds that we join the church when we make a profession of faith. A profession means two things. We usually think today about a profession as being like a statement, like making a declaration of faith. That we are going to walk with others though this life as best we can following Christ. But a profession also means an occupation. We often think of a profession as being like a job. Something specialized perhaps. Being a fisherman was many of the disciples' first profession. Then Jesus called them to a new kind of profession, the other kind. To follow him. They didn't ask what the educational requirements were. They dropped their nets and followed him.

Their profession wasn't anything fancy. It was simply to follow Jesus. They weren't anything fancy either. Throughout their lives, these disciples would mess up, miss the mark, would contradict themselves, they would try and keep children away from Jesus, and

Christian Followership

would end up denying him. They took all sorts of roundabout roads on their journey. But in the end, the roads led back to Jesus and they would follow Jesus.

Joining the church, being a Christian, making a profession of faith, means we do our best to follow Jesus. Just as we are. Where we are. As we are. It doesn't mean necessary one congregation or one creed or one expression of faith.

It's ok to ask big questions. God can handle the questions. I have struggled with some of the dogma of our faith tradition since my confirmation class when I was confirmed. I bet I am not alone.

Following Jesus doesn't mean staying super strong, always being perfect, not being scared, never sinning, or not falling, failing, or flailing about. The good news is that while you may disappoint yourself, if you keep following Jesus you will please him.

Being a Christian simply means we follow Jesus. To try and do what he does. Go where he does. Make his mission your mission. What you are saying as you join the church, much as it has been for so many for so long, is that you have a willingness, an openness, to follow Jesus where he leads you.

Jesus called the disciples. Our tradition holds that God calls us. Calls everyone. God has something for each of us. That our first calling, our initial identity, our first profession, is just to follow him.

You are called to be his disciple too.

Much as the disciples' activity took place around water, we join the covenant community through the waters of baptism.

We baptize because Jesus said we should. When Jesus was baptized, the holy spirit descended on him and God said, "this is my beloved, with whom I am well pleased." Beloved.

We don't baptize ourselves. Not even Jesus baptized himself. We receive baptism. At baptism we receive the grace of God.

It's a bit risky to express and profess one's faith. It's also exciting. The disciples dropped their nets. We think about nets sometimes as in safety nets. It was their livelihood, salary, or food in their case that they dropped. Who knows what it is that we need to drop?

Your identity in baptism, as a child of God who sees all other people as children of God too, is more important than any of the classifications and allegiances that can too easily divide us.

At confirmation we nurture the grace that is given at our baptism. Then we are called to spend our life sharing it with others.

Jesus calls his disciples to be "fishers of people." Jesus expresses this when he invites, when he calls, his disciples to be fishers of people. That means to share the love and grace of God with others so to include them in the family of grace.

Jesus fished for them. They were called in turn to fish for others.

We know from John 4 that the disciples did lots of baptizing, so that presumes they themselves were baptized.

They shared with others, what was done to them.

We all called as Christians to be fishers of people. That means that we do for others, to share with others, what Christ has done for us. Jesus fishes for the disciples. Now we are to fish for others by sharing the love we have received with others.

We don't baptize ourselves; we receive our baptism. We don't fish for ourselves; Jesus fishes for us. We don't call ourselves; Jesus calls us. We don't save ourselves; we receive salvation. We don't give ourselves God's grace, it is given to us through Christ.

We spend the rest of our lives sharing that grace, sharing it with others.

Now our challenge is to work throughout our life to share the grace we have been given with others.

Perhaps as we emerge from this year, this particular year, this Covid year, this season, we will find a bit of our purpose in our identity, in our calling, our realizing the why of God's purpose for our lives, and nurture God's grace.

Then as you go forward into discipleship, church membership, involvement, and leadership in the church of Jesus Christ, you might remember that you are called, first and foremost, in the end, to simply follow.

Follow the one who will get in the boat with you when the sea is rough.

Follow the one who calls you to drop your net and trust him.

Follow him into the adventure of faith. Follow him by doing something for someone else out of gratitude.

Follow the one who will journey along with you if you walk the road along with him.

Follow Jesus as his disciple. And have faith.

For he has faith in you too.

Let us pray. *Loving God, we know there are many roads we can take in life. Help us to find that they all come back in the end to your leading us to follow you. Amen.*

www.ingramcontent.com/pod-product-compliance
Lightning Source LLC
Chambersburg PA
CBHW070613010526
44118CB00012B/1498